GENDER MATTERS

*Female Policymakers'
Influence in Industrialized
Nations*

Valerie R. O'Regan

PRAEGER

Westport, Connecticut
London

Library of Congress Cataloging-in-Publication Data

O'Regan, Valerie R., 1956–
    Gender matters : female policymakers' influence in industrialized
nations / Valerie R. O'Regan.
        p.   cm.
    Includes bibliographical references and index.
    ISBN 0–275–96884–7 (alk. paper) ✓
    1. Women in politics.   2. Representative government and
representation.   3. Women—Government policy.   I. Title: Female
policymakers' influence in industrialized nations.   II. Title.
HQ1236 O69   2000
320'.082'0973—dc21   99–055879

British Library Cataloguing in Publication Data is available.

Library of Congress Catalog Card Number: 99–055879
ISBN: 0–275–96884–7

First published in 2000

Praeger Publishers, 88 Post Road West, Westport, CT 06881
An imprint of Greenwood Publishing Group, Inc.
www.praeger.com

Printed in the United States of America

The paper used in this book complies with the
Permanent Paper Standard issued by the National
Information Standards Organization (Z39.48–1984).

10 9 8 7 6 5 4 3 2 1

Contents

Illustrations   vii
Acknowledgments   ix

1. Introduction   1
   What Is Representation?   2

2. Women Representing Women   21
   Women's Interests   21
   Female Representation   22

3. The Current Study   29
   The First Analysis   30
   The Second Analysis   41

4. Comparing Equal Wage Policies   49
   North American Nations   49
   Commonwealth and Former Commonwealth Nations   52
   Mediterranean Nations   56
   Scandinavian Nations   60
   Other European Nations   64

Japan   69
Overview   71

5. Results of the Analyses   77
   The First Analysis   79
   The Second Analysis   98
   Discussion   114

6. Conclusion   119

Appendix   125
Bibliography   129
Index   151

Illustrations

FIGURES

4.1 Equal Wage Policies   74

5.1 Correlation Analysis for Analysis I (1960–1975)   85

5.2 Correlation Analysis for Analysis I (1976–1994)   85

5.3 Correlation Analysis for Analysis II (1960–1975)   104

5.4 Correlation Analysis for Analysis II (1976–1994)   105

TABLES

5.1 Means and Standard Deviations for Dependent Variables for Analysis I   82

5.2 Dependent Variable: Employment and Wage Protection Policy Parameter Estimates and Standard Errors   87

5.3 Dependent Variable: Social Policy w/Abortion Policy Parameter Estimates and Standard Errors   89

5.4 Dependent Variable: Social Policy Excluding Abortion Policy Parameter Estimates and Standard Errors   91

5.5 Means and Standard Deviations for Dependent Variables for Analysis II   102

5.6 Dependent Variable: Equal Wage Policy—Scale 1
     Parameter Estimates and Standard Errors   107

5.7 Dependent Variable: Equal Wage Policy—Scale 2
     Parameter Estimates and Standard Errors   108

Acknowledgments

I wish to express my appreciation and gratitude to those who made this work possible. To Professor Grace Saltzstein, whose guidance, patience, and support during this project were invaluable. To Professor Barbara Sinclair for her critical evaluation and useful comments. To Professor Shaun Bowler for his constant encouragement and practical attitude about completing the project. To Professor Will Moore for his assistance in the analysis of the data during his own hectic moving preparations.

I wish to thank Joan Littlejohn and Aline Messer for their support, assistance, and friendship during my years at U.C. Riverside. I also wish to thank my new department colleagues at North Dakota State University, including Jill Blazek, Bob Wood, John Monzingo, and Curtis Amlund for their encouragement and assistance.

Special thanks are due to "the cohort" composed of Greg Thorson, Olof Ronny Lindström, David McCuan, Chris McHorney, Carole Kennedy, Don Matthewson, and Craig Arceneaux for their encouragement and friendship during the years of graduate school and beyond.

My deepest appreciation is reserved for my family, including my husband Steve Stambough, my mother Rose, sisters Linda and Stephanie, brother Mike, brothers-in-law Ron and Gary, and my nieces Kayleigh and Veronica. Their encouragement has been a constant in my life. Furthermore, I would like to thank my in-laws, especially Angie, Joe, and Nancy.

Chapter 1

Introduction

Although women have become more politically educated and active over the years, the election of 1992 will go down in U.S. history as the first "Year of the Woman." During that election a record number of female candidates ran for and won their parties' nominations for national and state legislative seats. As a result of the increased opportunity to vote for viable female candidates, the number of women in the House of Representatives went from 29 to 47, the number of female Senators tripled (from two to six) and female members in state legislatures increased to 20 percent of all seats (Wilcox, 1994).

The resulting changes in the composition of the legislative bodies encouraged many to believe that, based on appearances, the system in the United States was becoming more representative of the population. Those reveling in the increased female legislative presence presumed that the government would move closer to exemplifying popular representation and, therefore, be more democratic. Yet we still know surprisingly little about the connections between female electoral representation and democracy. The purpose of this study is to contribute to the literature concerning the link between female representation and democracy by examining the relationship between female policymakers and policy outcome.

WHAT IS REPRESENTATION?

Scholars (Verba & Nie, 1972; Eulau & Prewitt, 1973; Tucker & Zeigler, 1980) note the connection between representative responsiveness to constituents' preferences and the existence of a democratic system of government. However, representation is not naturally linked to democracy; nations that provide some form of representation are not always democracies. Historically, the responsibility of representing the masses was not limited to individuals chosen or elected specifically for the task; often the responsibility was given by virtue of birthright. For example, kings represented their subjects in their decision making despite the fact the kings were not specifically selected to represent their subjects' interests. However, as a result of the American founders' efforts to develop a nation free of a monarchy, the term "representation" began to refer to popular representation and democratic government.

Indeed, in systems of representative democracy today assessments of how democratic the system is inevitably depend upon assessments of the nature and quality of representation. Hence, representation is now considered the crucial element of democracy in modern representative democracies.

Yet analysts and theorists have struggled for years to understand and explain what representation means or entails in a democratic system of government. Their research has progressed from vague perceptions of the actors' responsibilities in the representation relationship, to specific explanations of the reasons for and activities involved in the representation process.

Beginning with a discussion of Thomas Hobbes' treatment of representation and continuing through the development of further explorations of what representation entails, the seminal work of Hanna Pitkin (1967) offers three views of the concept of representation: formalistic, "standing for," and "acting for."

According to Pitkin, formalistic conceptions of representation refer to the formalities of the representation relationship. Two major formalistic approaches have been used to explain representation: the authorization view and the accountability view. According to the authorization view, the person acting as a delegate for the constituents is authorized to act for those being represented; the representative is free to act as she/he wants to in the relationship with no repercussions. The problem with this view of representation is that it does not address what constitutes representative activity or the reasons for representative decision making. Acting in the best interest or perceived best interest of the represented is not considered in this determination of representation; as a result, it cannot be determined if the representative is doing a good or bad job. Instead, the view concentrates on the delegate's authority or lack of authority to act for the represented. Furthermore, those being represented are responsible for the consequences of the representative's actions despite any disapproval they have for those actions (Pitkin, 1967, pp. 38–39).

The second formalistic approach, the accountability view, has a different perspective on the responsibility of the representative. Although this view shares the same formality of structure and lack of substantive content as the authorization view, the accountability view differs in its placement of responsibility. In comparison to the authorization view, the accountability approach holds the representative accountable for her/his own actions; as a result, the representative must answer to those she/he represents (Pitkin, 1967, p. 55).

Due to the formalistic views' limited clarification of what representation activity involves, advancements in representation theory introduced new definitions, including the "standing for" and "acting for" views. In associating representation with standing for a constituency, it is assumed that the representative shares similar characteristics with the represented (descriptive representation) or is considered a symbol of the group that is being represented (symbolic representation). In both cases the representative's personal characteristics rather than the actions taken by the representative determine the responsibility of representation. In descriptive representation the legitimacy of a representative is based on how accurately the representative resembles or reflects the constituency; hence, it is assumed that people's characteristics guide their decision making and the actions they take.

Symbolic representation involves emotional attachments to a representative rather than "rationally justifiable" connections. The response to such representative symbols "depends more on training and habit than on learning or understanding" (Pitkin, 1967, pp. 100–101). In as much as a country's flag symbolizes national unity and pride, this type of representation is based on symbolic value associated with a representative; how the people regard the representative establishes legitimacy.

As in descriptive representation, actions that determine the representative's commitment to the constituency are not pertinent for symbolic representation to occur. However, contrary to the descriptive type, symbolic representation lacks the assumption that a link exists between personal characteristics and decision making; the particular symbol that "stands for" or represents is not "a source of information" but a "recipient or object of feelings" (Pitkin, 1967, p. 99).

The other view that Pitkin addresses extensively is "acting for" or substantive representation. This view concentrates on the activity that goes on during representation rather than on the external similarity or symbolic importance of the representative to the target group. In this case a representative's behavior and responsibility for her/his constituents provides the explanation for representation and the link between the two groups of actors; actual representation rather than potential representation is analyzed. However, analysts have had a difficult time defining and measuring representative activity under this conception.

Besides Pitkin, other scholars have studied the relationship between the representative and the constituents and have distinguished representative behavior. Numerous scholars (Miller & Stokes, 1963; Wahlke, 1971; Verba & Nie, 1972; Luttbeg, 1974; Eulau & Karps, 1977; Tucker & Zeigler, 1980) have sought to examine the possible influence constituencies have over their representative's decision making.

The 1963 study by Miller and Stokes is considered to be one of the more innovative efforts at determining the relationship or "congruence" between representatives and constituents. Focusing more on constituency influence than on representation, Miller and Stokes argue that three conditions must be met for constituency control to occur. The first condition involves constituents choosing a representative with similar convictions to their own; therefore, the representative will act on his or her own convictions as well as on the constituents' convictions. The second condition is based on the representative's desire for reelection; constituents maintain control by basing their voting behavior on how the representative has worked for their interests. The final condition involves the constituency's responsibility to choose a representative based on the representative's policy views; it is expected that the constituency is informed and makes a decision based on that knowledge.

Miller and Stokes concluded that the communication necessary to convey information between the two parties is far from perfect; this results in both parties being unaware of the other's preferences and policy stands, lessening the possibility of influence. Although their focus on influence does not explain representation, the researchers demonstrate that communication between the representatives and constituents has a considerable effect on whether the representative responds to the constituents. The researchers also provide a more effective method of studying representation by interviewing constituents and their representatives. However, their method has been criticized for limiting the study of representation to the electoral connection.

Building on the work of Miller and Stokes, Eulau and Karps (1977) conceptualize representation to include factors other than the electoral process as potential influences on representatives' conduct. Eulau and Karps emphasize the complexity of representation and responsiveness. They argue that it includes four separate components. The four components are policy, service, allocation, and symbolic responsiveness. Policy responsiveness refers to the representative's attention to the important public issues of the time. Service responsiveness refers to efforts made by the representative to assist his or her constituents in their attempts to obtain government services. Allocation responsiveness involves the representative's use of pork-barrel exchanges or administrative interventions to benefit her/his constituency in the allocation of public goods. Lastly, symbolic responsiveness refers to the public gestures made by the representative to encourage the constituents' trust and support (Eulau & Karps, 1977, p. 241). Individually, these four components can be thought of as distinct targets or forms that responsiveness can take; combined, they provide a more complex, multidimensional view of representation.

Efforts to further the study of representation demonstrate the lack of consensus regarding the appropriate operationalization of responsiveness and representation. Attempts to conceptualize responsiveness by distinguishing activity that is applicable to the representation process and provides tangible measures of responsiveness include the use of legislative policy advocacy or support (Davidson, 1967), agenda setting based on discussion topics (Tucker & Ziegler, 1980), opportunities for public participation (Tucker & Ziegler, 1980), policy development (Karnig, 1975), and policy implementation (Schumaker & Loomis, 1979).

Other efforts address interest and priority agreement between the representative and the represented; this research investigates how well representative decision making corresponds to the constituents' preferences. Such efforts have conceptualized responsiveness as concurrence between representatives' policy agendas and constituency priorities (Verba & Nie, 1972) or as policy outcomes that conform to the needs of the target group (Dresang, 1974).

As noted, there is a lack of consensus regarding what type of activity is appropriate to conceptualize responsiveness. One type of activity may be considered more symbolic, another type, more real. Issue advocacy and opportunities for public participation can appear more symbolic than real. Representatives publicly advocating or supporting an issue can lead constituents to believe that their interests are shared. Constituents can also assume that they are being represented if they are encouraged to participate and voice their opinions in public. However, neither of these activities guarantee that representatives are acting in the best interest of the represented or are listening to constituents' opinions.

On the other hand, activities like agenda setting, policy development, and policy implementation suggest more commitment on the part of the representative, and thus, more responsiveness. However, these activities may be the result of other factors, such as party support or economic conditions, rather than a response to constituent demands. The results of the studies may also differ depending on the level of controversy surrounding the agenda or policy. Legislative agendas addressing less controversial issues, such as anticrime and antitaxation policies, generate shared support among representatives and constituents; as a result these are safer issues for representatives to endorse. Conversely, the more controversial issues, such as abortion rights, affirmative action, or homosexual rights, test the commitment level of the representative since advocacy of these issues could result in a decline of party and electoral support.

Besides the difficulty of operationalizing responsiveness, it is also a complicated task to determine concurrence and conformity between the opinions and preferences of the two groups of actors: representatives and their constituents. Deciding which opinions are pertinent in determining concurrence is a difficult process. In addition, measuring concurrence is not a simple task. As research (Gormley et al., 1983) suggests, utilizing a more complex method to measure concurrence, rather than relying on the use of a single measure such as agreement on issue prioritizing, may be needed for an adequate assessment of the concept. Despite the difficulties, researchers (Verba & Nie, 1972; Gormley et al., 1983) conclude that the use of concurrence is helpful in comparing the attitudes of the different participants; however, it is less helpful in making comparisons between attitudes and policies since concurrence only measures the possibility of responsiveness, not the actual policy responsiveness.

In addition to the complexity of defining the concepts, problems with the direction of responsiveness have appeared when dealing with concurrence. To measure concurrence between leaders and constituents by focusing on problem priorities, Verba and Nie (1972) analyzed the relationships between "leader activism" and concurrence and "citizen activism" and concurrence. Since the researchers found the correlation coefficients stronger for the citizens than those for the leaders, they concluded that their concurrence measure appeared to accurately measure "responsiveness to leaders" (Verba & Nie, 1972, pp. 331–332). However, the coefficients, which were positive for both citizens and leaders, failed to indicate the direction of causality. Citizens may influence leaders and/or leaders may influence citizens.

Miller and Stokes' research on constituency control, related to attitudinal and perceptual congruence (1963) encounters the same direction problem. The results do not indicate if the information that must be communicated to determine congruence is transmitted from the constituency to the representative or vice versa. Their research also lacks controls for other forces, such as party influence, that can affect representation. Thus, to further the analysis of the relationship between representatives and constituents, research needs to control for other factors that could explain the results.

In addition to research examining the relationship between representatives and the general population, further analysis targets specific groups of citizens. Studies have examined the representation of select groups in the population by representatives who share characteristics and interests with the citizens in the group. One area of study concentrates on the representation of African Americans and other minorities. Research examining the representation of African American constituents by African American policymakers approaches the subject from both the descriptive/standing for (e.g., Karnig, 1976; Meier & Nigro, 1976; Cayer & Sigelman, 1980) and the substantive/acting for (e.g., Welch & Karnig, 1979; Eisinger, 1982) points of view.

Most of the early work focused on the general analysis of African Americans achieving fair representation, whereby the proportion of black representatives equals the proportion of blacks in the population. Because this research was based on the appearance rather than the outcome of representation, further studies were needed to address the actual activity of representation.

Studies investigating the substantive effects of African American representation produce mixed results. A portion of the research demonstrates a commitment to, and prioritizing of, issues that are presumed to be important to African American constituents. According to Conyers and Wallace (1976) and Thomas (1991b), black representatives feel a commitment to serving their minority constituents; this commitment results in the prioritizing of policies that concern the targeted constituency. For example, housing and education issues tend to be priorities of black elected officials, reflecting their concern for the disadvantaged groups in their community (Cole, 1976). Other research provides evidence that African American mayors are influential when dealing with employment issues; according to Eisinger (1982) and Saltzstein (1989), the level of minority employment has increased as a result of the presence of African American mayors.

However, the commitment of African American representatives to issues benefiting their minority constituencies is not as apparent in other studies. One examination of black city officials discovered that black mayors allocate more funding for social welfare programs and less for protective services and physical facilities (Welch & Karnig, 1979). Although social welfare is important to African Americans, the same can be said for protective services since crime and fire statistics are high in poorer neighborhoods that are inhabited by large African American populations. Furthermore, Keller (1978) notes that black mayors do not automatically prioritize funding for welfare programs or community services differently than white mayors do. Therefore, it appears problematic to expect certain public expenditures to be more important to a group of citizens based on the citizens' race.

Aside from the research on African American representatives, a minimal amount of research has been done on the representation of other minority groups, primarily focusing on the Latino population. These studies show similar results. Due to the lack of Latino representatives at the state and national levels, most of the research examines local level officials. One study reveals that the level of Latino school board members has a positive effect on the employment of Latino teachers, the educational environment of Latino students, and the likelihood of Latino students attending college (Fraga et al., 1986). Other research that examines Latino city council members finds the level of representation significantly affects the level of Latino employment in the city (Dye & Renick, 1981).

Due to the limited amount of research on the substantive influence of minority representatives, there is a lack of strong evidence to support the presumption that minority representatives will be especially responsive to their minority constituents. It is also difficult to measure this responsiveness since the benefits of public policies are not limited to specific racial groups and, therefore, cannot be categorized as strictly African American, Latino, or Caucasian policies. For example, both black and white mayors know the importance of social welfare and community service programs for their constituents (Keller, 1978).

It is also difficult to isolate the effect of minority representation from other factors on policy outcomes. Researchers point out that, although minority city officials have an effect on minority employment, a better predictor of minority employment is the percentage of the minority population (Eisinger, 1982; Stein, 1986). In addition, other socioeconomic factors like income and education levels need to be controlled when determining what actually affects policy that is beneficial to minority populations.

Besides analyzing the effects of minority representation on minority constituents, other studies address labor and class-based influences on policy making. Studies on the influence of labor assert that representatives linked to labor movements support policies that protect workers' pensions and employment. Here we find the money and membership that unions represent sway decisions made by policymakers toward legislation that is important to unions. For example, organized labor's influence helped establish portions of the Social Security Act in the United States (Berg, 1994).

Research on the British system demonstrates competing unions' power in the workplace and in Parliament to manipulate and block industrial policy for the preferred outcomes (Heidenheimer et al., 1990). Kohl (1981) proposes that nations with strong union influence lead in welfare spending, resulting in general public expenditure increases.

Although studies show that unions in the United States were capable of influencing representatives in the past, union influence has weakened over time due to declining membership. With the decline in union influence, representatives are turning to other sources for monetary and voter support, such as large corporations and other interest groups with a more conservative ideology; this has resulted in representatives promoting the interests of the new sources of support (Berg, 1994).

Besides racial and labor influence, studies suggest that class bias also influences public policy. Researchers propose both indirect and direct effects. An indirect effect can be found in popular voting. Those who make up the electorate are more representative of the upper class (Burnham, 1987) since voter decline has been concentrated in the lower-class population (Burnham, 1982; Piven & Cloward, 1989). Some have argued that this class bias within the electorate has resulted in public policies that reward the upper class (Piven & Cloward, 1989) and in lower levels of redistributive policies (Hill & Leighley, 1992).

Along with the overrepresentation of the wealthy in the electorate, many analysts argue (Stanley et al., 1967; Prewitt & Stone, 1973; Dye, 1979; Davidson & Oleszek, 1994) that the potential for class bias within government exists, resulting in a direct effect on public policies. Analyses of representation reveal that those elected or appointed to government office are more likely to be part of the socially privileged classes. Besides similarities in age, education, and occupation, the average representative tends to be part of the economic elite (Dye, 1979; Davidson & Oleszek, 1994; Keefe & Ogul, 1997). Therefore, analysts contend, class status influences the views and priorities of those in policy-making positions (Burnham, 1987).

However, contrary to this contention, researchers note that the economic class of the representative has less to do with policy-making decisions than do other factors, such as the party or religious affiliation of the policymaker (Davidson & Oleszek, 1994; Keefe & Ogul, 1997). In addition, Miller and Stokes (1963) claim that representatives are conscious of the policy preferences and electoral power of their constituents and will act in the constituents' best interest to maintain their voting support; all this despite the fact that the representative's constituents may be lower or middle class. However, as Miller and Stokes demonstrate, this electoral relationship between representatives and constituents is burdened by imperfect information and lack of awareness.

In addition to race, labor, and class influences, many analysts expect that the sex of the representative can influence policy outcome. Expecting women to be more sensitive to the issues that concern them and to have an effect on policy consequences dates back to the early 1900s. At that time advocates of female suffrage predicted that the choices women would make in the voting booths would result in policies addressing issues such as world peace, child labor, injustices attributed to the urban political machine, and temperance (Hansen, 1995). Though early research failed to demonstrate the predicted influence between women's suffrage and policy consequences that opponents and supporters of suffrage anticipated, researchers maintained that women would have more influence on policy outcomes as women became more involved in the political process through their voting behavior, political activity, and election or appointment to political office. Based on this expectation, scholars were encouraged to analyze the course of female political involvement over the years.

To date, research relating to women and politics has focused primarily on the limited presence or absence of women in the political arena, with particular emphasis on the relative paucity of women holding political office. In the United States, female membership in the House of Representatives has lingered at the 5 percent level throughout the 1970s and 1980s. The 1990s brought an increase of female representation to the 10 percent level. For the same time period, female representation in the Senate has remained in the single digits, ranging from no female senators in the mid-1970s, to 2 percent during the 1980s, to a peak of 6 percent female membership in 1993.

In the Western European nations, we find some differences in the level of female legislative representation. The Scandinavian nations show an earlier presence and increase of female legislators, with the percentage averaging 6 percent in the 1950s, 12 percent in the mid-1960s, 21 percent in the mid-1970s, and 32 percent in the mid-1980s. Female legislative membership in other Western European nations ranges from 2 percent in the early 1970s to 20 percent by the late 1980s.

For the top government positions, there have been only 32 female heads of state or government throughout the world; half of these positions were acquired since 1990. Furthermore, female cabinet membership has remained at a low or nonexistent level through the years. Currently, women hold a little over 6 percent of the world's cabinet positions, an increase from the 3.3 percent of the positions held in 1987. Scholars interested in the topic have pointed to institutional/structural factors, social roles, and demographics as primary correlates of observed low levels of female officeholding.

Institutional or structural factors that have been implicated in female underrepresentation include electoral systems, parties, incumbency, and eligibility pools. According to the electoral system research, single-member district systems hinder female representation while proportional representation systems result in greater percentages of female representation (Duverger, 1955; Castles, 1981; Lovenduski & Hills, 1981; Norris, 1985; Rule, 1987; Welch & Studlar, 1990). Further research investigates the influence of political parties on female political underrepresentation (Haavio-Mannila et al., 1985; Norris, 1987; Darcy et al., 1987). Scholars argue that left-wing parties, including socialist, communist, and Christian parties, are more committed to nominating and supporting female candidates. Others suggest that certain party activities, such as establishing quotas (Rule & Norris, 1992) and selecting women for political appointments (Darcy et al., 1987; Dahlerup, 1988), can influence female representation.

Besides the electoral system and party influence, research on the incumbency advantage (Jacobson, 1990) and the female eligibility pool (Bullock & Heys, 1972; Martin, 1989) offer further explanations of why there are so few female representatives. The incumbency advantage provides name recognition, financial support, and free campaigning benefits to the candidate holding the office; with these advantages, it is difficult for a candidate to lose an election. As more women get elected and run for reelection, the incumbency advantage will work for them rather than against them.

When selecting a candidate to run for office or be appointed to a government position, parties and officeholders make their selection from a candidate pool. Those included in this pool have the education, occupation, and/or political experience that make them quality candidates. In the past the socialization process limited female access to the necessary educational, occupational, and political opportunities (Darcy et al., 1987). As a result women were not part of the candidate pool from which eligible candidates were selected. However, as women acquire the education and experience to be considered viable candidates and appointees, the number of women in the eligibility pool will increase.

Societal views of women and the social roles associated with females in the population are also factors identified as barriers to the electability and representation of women. According to various researchers, women are apolitical. Their concerns tend to involve the nurturance and care of the family and society (Berelson et al., 1954; Campbell et al., 1960) to the exclusion of political concerns. Others claim that women lack the necessary traits to be successful in political life; since women are considered to be nonaggressive and unambitious, they are judged to be unsuited for political activity (Mandel, 1981; Sapiro, 1983; Leeper, 1991). These studies contend that traits associated with women, such as passivity and emotional behavior, are to be blamed for women's inability to succeed in politics.

Finally, the demographics of the electorate have been used to explain female underrepresentation. According to the voting behavior literature, voter class, education level, religious commitment, sex, and race (Schneider & Smith, 1973; Ferree, 1974; Bernstein & Polly, 1975; Welch & Sigelman, 1982; Sigelman & Sigelman, 1982) all influence perceptions of the viability and competence of women in the political process. Studies suggest that voters who are middle or upper class, better educated, less frequent church attenders, female, and African American are more accepting of female candidates.

This knowledge has helped to motivate women and women's groups to take advantage of political systems and party activities that benefit female participation, to challenge perceptions that limit women in the political process, and to mobilize specific groups in the population to support female candidates. As a result of these actions more women have become politically involved and the number of female representatives has increased.

In the United States, evidence of this change in female political involvement can be found in the 1992 election. Due to the increase of open seats resulting from a record number of incumbent retirements, the perception that male government officials

ignore the problems women face in society,[1] and the mobiliza-
tion of voters angered by the apparent shortage of female representation, a record number of women ran for public office
(Wilcox, 1994). During the election, there were 218 female congressional candidates running in the primaries in comparison to
the previous record of 134 in 1986. Partially due to the increase
in female candidates, 119 female candidates won their party's
nomination and ran in the general elections (108 for House seats
and 11 for Senate seats). As a result of the larger female candidate pool and other circumstances surrounding the election, the
number of female House members increased and the number of
female senators tripled, as mentioned earlier.

Besides the late entry of women into politics and the sluggish
increase of female officeholders, research indicates that the female influence has been delayed in other realms of political activity. The opinion that women were not interested in politics,
rarely voted or participated, and when they did vote, voted like
their husbands, prevailed through the years. Most of the early
theoretical work viewed women as apolitical (Figes, 1970; Mahowald, 1978; Pateman, 1980) and therefore, lacking the necessary qualities for participation in the civic community.
Research through the 1960s maintained that women lacked political interest, resulting in their desire to avoid political involvement (Berelson et al., 1954; Campbell et al., 1960).

In the 1970s, feminist scholars offered reasons for the earlier
conclusions. Jane Jaquette (1974) and others (Bourque & Gros-
holtz, 1974) suggested that the earlier research was an inaccurate
portrayal of female political behavior due to theoretical biases
and methodological problems. Because of these biases and problems, the legitimate differences between women and men were
exaggerated, and women were judged to be apolitical based on
male political behavior being the norm.

During the 1970s and 1980s, research shifted away from the
notion that women were apolitical and uninterested in political
involvement to the examination of similarities between women
and men in political activity. Studies indicated that women were

as likely as men to vote, work on political campaigns, contribute money to candidates, attend political meetings, and write letters to public officials (Welch, 1977; Carroll, 1979; Baxter & Lansing, 1980; Beckwith, 1986). Others found that the increased female political participation was related to women acquiring a higher level of education (Welch, 1977; Sapiro, 1983), having fewer children (Jennings & Niemi, 1981; Sapiro, 1983) and working outside of the home (Andersen, 1975; Welch, 1977).

As research provided further evidence of comparability between male and female political participation at the grassroots level, the research of the 1980s and 1990s advanced the analysis of differences between the sexes that influence political decision making. Bennett and Bennett (1989) concluded that women were motivated to vote for different reasons than men. Women vote because they believe it is their civic responsibility, while men vote because they are interested in the election. As for vote choices, Welch and Hibbing (1992) found that women base their voting decisions on sociotropic economic considerations; on the other hand, men's egocentric economic decisions determine their voting choices.

According to the recent women and politics literature, women appear equally active and influential when it comes to voting for, supporting, and holding policymakers accountable for their actions. Furthermore, women are attaining these coveted policymaking positions at an increasing rate. Although increased female representation matters in the descriptive sense, many analysts argue that the true importance of increased female participation in policy making is in its substantive effects. Studies demonstrating differences both between female and male priorities and consequent voting decisions suggest a link between descriptive representation and substantive representation.

In addition, if the interests of women are distinct from those of men, the differences may be reflected in policy outcomes. Throughout Western history, male activities have been focused outside of the home and family in the male-established political community, whereas female activities have revolved around motherhood, housework, and basic subsistence work. As noted, in many societies activities associated with females have been labeled women's issues and have held less importance in policy making; as a result fewer resources and effort have been given to the formulation and implementation of policies of interest to women.

A few societies, primarily the Scandinavian nations, consider issues such as family service, day care, education, and medical services to be national interests rather than women's interests (Sainsbury, 1988). Thus, both female and male policy makers rank these policies as important services for the entire population and give such policies high priority.

Besides the Scandinavian countries, studies of other nations maintain that, even though these issues are labeled women's issues, male representatives are as willing and as capable as female representatives to work for them. This research contends that the better determinants of policy prioritizing are representative party affiliation (Haavind, 1982; Lovenduski, 1993) and the socioeconomic conditions of the nation under analysis (Norris, 1987). Further evidence of the lack of disparity between female and male policy priorities is found in Mezey (1978) and Norris and Lovenduski (1989). Both studies argue that female and male candidates and policymakers support the same political issues.

In addition to this research, other studies contend that policy priorities and leadership style are not dependent on gender but on ambition; female representatives support the same policies and act in the same manner as their male counterparts do to gain influence and reelection. This is particularly true in nations with small percentages of female policymakers. However, as the percentages of female representatives increase to what many refer to as a "critical level," it is expected that women will influence policy outcomes to reflect women's interests (Lovenduski, 1986; Dahlerup, 1988). It is also expected that as women acquire and maintain policy-making positions for extended periods of time, they will accumulate the seniority needed to be influential. For example, Noelle Norton (1995) explains that in the U.S. Congress, female members are limited in their committee and sub-committee assignments due to a lack of seniority; as a result their influence over policy formulation is also limited. As more women acquire key committee positions, their influence over women's interest policies will grow.

Looking at the big picture, with more women achieving political office, opportunities to determine if they have an effect on the political process increase. To analyze the effect of female policymakers, it is useful to determine any attitudinal differences based on sex that influence the prioritizing of issues and result in policies reflective of this prioritizing. Some argue that citizens' needs and requirements for public services transcend gender; however, others contend that there are specific issues that affect women more than men. Researchers examining these differences find an obvious gender gap in voting behavior and public opinion that is attributed to differences in values and priorities between men and women (Frankovic, 1982; Norris, 1985; Shapiro & Mahajan, 1986; Conover, 1988). Issues dealing with employment equality, compassion toward the disadvantaged, protection from domestic violence, care for the elderly and children, and protection from exploitation tend to reflect these differences, with women consistently ranking these issues as more worthy of attention than do men (Sapiro, 1981; Shapiro & Mahajan, 1986; Huddy & Terkildsen, 1993).

Moreover, those examining women in government assert that female policymakers prioritize these issues differently than their male counterparts do because gender influences an understanding of how important these issues are. Whatever the cause, we might reasonably expect such pronounced differences in policy priorities to be reflected in policy outcomes as the percentage of female policymakers increases.

This study attempts to detect such a relationship through analysis of the relationship between representation of female policymakers and the existence or absence of two types of policy assumed to be important to women: employment and wage protection policy and social policy.

NOTE

1. The image of an all-male Senate panel questioning Anita Hill about her sexual harassment charges against Clarence Thomas appalled many women. This in turn motivated women to become involved by voting, contributing time and money, and running for office to bring the female perspective to government.

Chapter 2 _____

Women Representing Women

WOMEN'S INTERESTS

The first step is to determine the types of issues that are considered more important to women than to men. Virginia Sapiro (1981) argues that women's interests encompass "the expansion of rights, liberties, and opportunities for women where these have been denied or inhibited in comparison with those of men" (Sapiro, 1991, p. 705). Sapiro and others (Thomas & Welch, 1991; Thomas, 1991a) find that women often put a higher priority on issues involving the private (especially the domestic) sphere of the female social life, with special significance associated with the nurturing, protection, and support of the family and children. Walker (1986) suggests that women's concerns are not limited to the family but encompass the responsibility and care of all human beings.

Irene Diamond and Nancy Hartsock (1981) argue that what women consider important is something totally different than what men consider important. These interests include reproductive freedom and abortion rights. Furthermore, women tend to be more supportive of education, social welfare, and public health than do their male counterparts (Mezey, 1978; Darcy et al., 1987). In other words, women's interests not only deal with the family but also with society; services in the health and education fields that nurture and protect people have been shown to be of high priority to women.

This differential in male/female priorities is presumed to result from the sexual division of labor; women in the aggregate are held more responsible than men for the care of children and the family (Kelly et al., 1991). Whatever the source, numerous analysts argue, issue differences between women and men are intensified by male/female differentials in political participation and influence, ultimately reflected in law and public policy. Hence, for example, governmental policies regarding marital status, protection from violence, control over fertility, family responsibilities, and employment and educational opportunities all have elements that have been linked with male preferences, priorities, and interests (Sapiro, 1981).

As noted, numerous analysts support the argument that women's issues or interests do exist. Though the definitions regarding these issues or interests vary somewhat among researchers, most analysts contend that women tend to be most interested in issues that deal with nurturance and protection of children and with the family and society as a whole.

FEMALE REPRESENTATION

If women in general attach higher priority to certain issues than do men, can we expect women in government to attach higher priority to these issues than do their male counterparts? Furthermore, if such issues are more important to women in general and to women in government, will women in policy-making positions be more likely than their male counterparts to "act on" these issues to make them public policy?

The question here is whether female representation in government is needed to represent identifiable women's interests in policy making or whether male policymakers might still represent women's concerns. Though the need for electoral support might encourage greater sensitivity on the part of male legislators to the interests of female voters, critics argue that male/female attitudinal differences make it less likely that male legislators will even perceive the existence of such interests. Furthermore, some argue, "only women can act for women in identifying *invisible* problems" that affect women's lives (Diamond & Hartsock, 1981, p. 720).

To answer these questions, we must first determine if female policymakers are naturally (due to their sex) more responsive to female concerns despite the diversity of these concerns. Debates surround this issue of responsiveness.

Initial studies of female officeholders challenged the assumption that women are apolitical by revealing female presence and activity in the political arena. Jeane Kirkpatrick's study of 50 female state legislators demonstrated that a "political woman exists" (Kirkpatrick, 1974, p. 220). Her research also noted that the female legislators included in the study were similar in social background and psychological characteristics to their male counterparts. However, this early research lacked further analysis of the significance of female representation beyond the descriptive and symbolic importance.

Beyond the initial research, scholars have focused on attitudinal differences and policy impact attributed to the sex of the legislator. Studies by the Center for the American Woman and Politics (1977, 1981, 1988) found different political attitudes and priorities between women and men regardless of their ideological perspectives. Women tend to demonstrate more liberal and feminist views than do their male counterparts despite political party affiliation (Frankovich, 1977; Leader, 1977; Thomas, 1989; Dodson, 1989). These liberal attitudes are expected to influence female values and interests in the private and public spheres.

Other studies analyze the effects of the different attitudes and priorities by examining the impact of female policymakers on policy outputs at different government levels; these studies produce various findings. At the local level, research demonstrates that women bring a different slant to male-dominated government. Some studies (Mezey, 1978; Merritt, 1980; Welch & Bledsoe, 1985) reveal that female city councilors are supportive of women's issues and are more egalitarian when it comes to de-fining male and female roles; however, Mezey (1978) found very little difference in issue prioritizing between female and male council members.

Analysis of the impact of female mayors is insufficient to make a general assessment about the female influence on city policy due to the scarcity of female mayors and the lack of opportunity to study their impact. However, the limited research suggests that a female mayor may contribute to employment equity by increasing female representation in municipal government jobs (Saltzstein, 1989).

At the state level, various studies conclude that female policymakers are influential in the policy-making process (Mezey, 1978; Saint-Germain, 1989; Reingold, 1990; Thomas & Welch, 1991). Many of these studies contend that female legislators are more likely to initiate and support legislation that focuses on women, children, and family issues (Werner, 1968; Diamond, 1977; Gehlen, 1977; Saint-Germain, 1989; Reingold, 1990; Thomas & Welch, 1991). Other studies claim that female legislators are more liberal than their male colleagues (Frankovic, 1977; Leader, 1977; Welch, 1985; Thomas, 1990) resulting in their support for policies that are reflective of this liberal inclination. However, some say that the attitudinal difference between the sexes is apparent in certain states and absent in others (Reingold, 1992). In several cases where there is evidence of an impact on policy output, researchers emphasize that it is necessary to reach a "critical or tilt level" of representation to affect the policy outcome; however, the critical level is not precisely defined (Saint-Germain, 1989; Thomas, 1992; Berkman & O'Connor, 1993).

Attempting to study the effect of female representation at the national level has been problematic due to the small sample size.[1] The limited amount of research suggests that female members of Congress support feminist policies and are more liberal in their voting than are male members (Leader, 1977; Frankovic,

1977, Welch, 1985), although party affiliation is a stronger predictor of voting. Liberal attitudes on the part of female representatives are particularly strong in policy areas such as
marijuana legalization, gun control, capital punishment, reproductive freedom, and foreign policy (Erikson & Luttbeg, 1973;
Diamond, 1977; Baxter & Lansing, 1980).

Beyond policy voting behavior, we find a further problem with
the lack of female influence at the initial stages of policy development. Since many of the female representatives are relative
newcomers to the national policy-making process, female membership on the appropriate congressional committees and sub-
committees is deficient. Between 1973 and 1992, the average
number of female members for certain committees was the following: Judiciary, 1.3; Appropriations, 2.1; Energy and Commerce, 1.1; and Education and Labor, 1.2. Thus, it appears that
women lack the influential positions in Congress and institutional
resources to transform women's issues into policy (Norton,
1995).

Studies at the international level address the question of
whether female officeholders influence policy in countries other
than the United States. The bulk of the research centers on the
Scandinavian nations because of their higher percentages of female representatives. Between 1970 and 1990, female legislative
representation ranged from 14 percent to 38 percent in the four
main Scandinavian nations (excluding Iceland) while female cabinet representation ranged from 6 percent to 45 percent (Haavio-
Mannila, 1985; Snyder, 1992).

Researchers working in this context find that female legislators
prioritize issues differently than male legislators do (Skard, 1980;
Sinkkonen & Haavio-Mannila, 1981; Skard & Haavio-Mannila,
1984; Dahlerup, 1988). According to these studies, women focus
primarily on social welfare, family law, child care, equality between the sexes, health, and education. From the research, we
find similar policy priorities focused on women's issues that transcend national boundaries. It also appears that female public of-

ficials in the Scandinavian nations feel it is their distinct obligation to represent the female portion of their constituency (Norderval, 1985).

Researchers have also expanded their inquiry to study the female influence on policy in developed nations, including Canada, Australia, New Zealand, Japan, and European nations (Sanzone, 1984; Norris & Lovenduski, 1989). The main problem faced by these researchers corresponds to the problem faced by those who study the system in the United States, namely, not enough female policymakers to study. The lack of a critical level of female policymakers has hindered the efforts of those seeking to study the female influence on policy prioritization and implementation within these nations.

In addition to the inadequate number of female subjects to study, other general problems exist throughout the literature. The lack of an agreed upon categorization of women's interests and policies at the local, state, national, and international levels contributes to the varying results. As mentioned earlier a pattern exists regarding the types of issues that are labeled important to women; however, the differing results demonstrate that some of the issues may be considered higher-priority women's issues or national issues rather than women's issues. Other factors may also influence the importance that female policymakers place on specific issues, such as dominant religious affiliation or regional conservatism affecting support for reproductive freedom policies.

Another problem with the existing research is the lack of a uniform definition of policy impact. The literature utilizes several different means of political activity to study the hypothesized influence of female officeholders on public policy; these include professional lobbying and voicing support for the policy, legislative voting for the passage of the policy, actual passage of the policy and examining the effectiveness of the implemented policy. Because the various studies analyze different activities, the results may not be considered comparable.

Finally, measurement of the policies is problematic. Researchers have utilized a dichotomous measure signifying the presence or absence of a policy, the assignment of values to specific characteristics of the policy, and/or descriptive statistics associated with the policy outcome. Due to the lack of a consistent method of measuring the breadth of the policy, the application of different measures results in noncomparable findings.

In recent years we find the percentage of female representation in policy-making positions increasing throughout the industrialized world. Although these nations still lack the representation levels found in the Scandinavian nations, the percentage of female policymakers in many of the nations is reaching double digits. Since 1990, 21 percent of the legislature and 20 percent of the cabinet in Germany have been female; in the Netherlands, 27 percent of the members of parliament and 24 percent of the cabinet have been women. The growth of female representation in recent years provides an opportunity to expand this area of research through a comparative international analysis of female legislators and policy.

In addition to expanding the analysis to compare female legislative behavior in the industrialized nations, this study utilizes two distinct methods of measuring the policy variables. As mentioned, measurement inconsistency is believed to be an influential factor in the variation of results; therefore, the use of two methods presents two separate opportunities to analyze the theorized relationship and note differing results. The first method involves three scales to measure the presence or absence of five individual policies categorized in two general policy areas. The second method involves two additional scales measuring the policy characteristics of one specific policy: equal wage policy. Furthermore, the general policy scales are constructed to separate two distinct policy categories: employment and wage protection policy and social policy. The purpose of separating the policies is to determine possible differences in the support of the two types of policy due to national or cultural conditions.

If women who achieve policy-making positions in government bring with them gender-related qualities and perceptions that they use to prioritize their policy decisions,[2] we would expect to see changes in policy output coinciding with changes in female representation. Hence, as women become more influential in the policy-making process through increased representation in legislatures around the world, their prioritizing of so-called women's issues should result in the formulation of public policies that address these concerns. Therefore, this study examines the relationship between the percentage of female representation in the industrialized nations and policy outputs.

NOTES

1. *The American Woman 1992–1993* (Ries & Stone, 1992) notes that in 1975, women made up 4 percent of the national legislature; in 1987, 5 percent of the legislature was female; and in 1991, 6 percent of the legislature was female.

2. This is despite other factors that may influence policy prioritizing, such as political ideology, religious affiliation, constituency, and so forth.

Chapter 3

The Current Study

This current study is composed of separate analyses addressing two possible effects that the number of female policymakers could have on the creation of public policy. The first analysis examines the relationship between the number of female policymakers in a country and the presence or absence of a variety of policies of special interest to women. The second analysis focuses on the relationship between the proportion of female policymakers and the presence and comprehensiveness of one specific policy, equal wage legislation, that is assumed to be highly important to women.

As noted earlier, previous research examining the effect of female policymakers on legislation and policy has been limited primarily to studying the effect of female representation on a limited array of policies in single nations. Those attempting to examine the effect in a broader, comparative sense have focused on policymaking in the small groups of nations that have larger proportions of female policymakers, mainly the Scandinavian nations. However, these comparisons are often criticized for being nongeneralizable; region-specific characteristics like early female participation in the labor force or welfare state orientation are suspected to be the actual determining factors. Further comparisons made among larger, more diverse groups of nations are nonexistent. Therefore, the logical progression of this research is to expand the number of countries and examine the relationship in a more comprehensive fashion.

THE FIRST ANALYSIS

The first analysis presented here extends previous research considerably by expanding the analysis to a cross-national sample of 22 nations and by examining the effect of female representation on two general types of policy that are important to women: employment and wage protection policy and social policy. Utilization of a larger cross-national sample allows us to address concerns that previously demonstrated gender effects on policy might actually have been due to country-specific characteristics (such as type of government in power, gross national product, presence of a welfare state, strength of the church, etc.). By including multiple countries that vary on such features, the effect of gender will be better supported if the adoption of policies dealing with women's issues still can be shown to be significantly linked with the increase of female legislators after controlling for such factors.

However, we cannot account for all possible economic and political distinctions at this time; instead the study proposed is to be limited to 22 industrialized, capitalist democracies.[1] By excluding socialist countries, the study avoids having to control for dictatorial and totalitarian regimes, government direction in their economies, and the economic and political conditions that result from these factors. Similarly, excluding third world countries eliminates the need to control for poverty levels, domestic conflict, external intervention, political instability, and repression prevalent in these countries. All 22 of the nations chosen held open elections and had open party competition during the entire time period used in this study, with the exception of Greece, Portugal, and Spain. As these three countries were not democracies continuously throughout this time span, the study will include only those years during which the three countries were under democratic rule and held open elections. The time period under examination is from

1960 to 1994, allowing 35 years to observe conditions and changes that occur, such as increases or decreases in female representation, coinciding with adoption of the specific policies.

Dependent Variables

Again, for this analysis, the dependent variables are interval-level measures of the presence or absence of a variety of policies in two broad areas of interest to women: employment and wage protection policy and social policy. The employment and wage protection policy variable consists of laws that focus on employment equality, protection of job status, and better working conditions in the work place. The social policy variable includes policies that establish and protect individual's rights in regard to marriage, education, and reproductive freedom.

By separating the two types of policy for analysis, we may be able to clear up some confusion in the extant literature[2] and be able to look for possible differences in the development of, and support for, the two types of policy. For example, employment and wage equality policies may command attention in those countries with high rates of female labor force participation. An example of this can be found in the Nordic countries where, due to the large percentage of women in the labor force, policies that address maternity leave, parental leave, and day care are viewed as national interests benefiting the entire population. Support for social policy, however, may have little to do with workforce participation but instead be linked with cultural or religious factors more or less supportive of sexual equality within the marriage and family structure.

As operationalized here, the employment and wage protection policy variable counts the presence or absence of equal wage policy, equal opportunity for women in employment policy, maternity leave policy, parental leave policy, and child care policy in each year in each country. The objective of all five of these policies is to target a problem or obligation dealing with employment that specifically affects women more than men. Legislating for equality of wages and employment opportunities addresses the wage disparity and job segregation issues that many (England & Norris, 1985; Jenson, 1995) insist need correction if equal status in the workplace is to be a reality. Maternity leave policy provides employment protection for women in their childbearing years. Parental leave allows for a partial shift of the responsibility for postnatal care to the father. It also provides job protection for either parent utilizing the leave opportunities. Child care policies provide various methods of monetary compensation, establishment of subsidized child care facilities, and/or job protection for the parent (the mother in most cases) who has the main responsibility for the upbringing of children. Depending on the nation, child care policies can provide one of these services or a combination of them. For example, child care policies in Ireland provide job protection with unpaid leave and subsidized services (Gauthier, 1996) while policies in Finland and France provide paid leave, job protection, and subsidized services (Kamerman & Kahn, 1991). Although the extent, support, and effectiveness of the individual policies vary across the nations, this part of the study does not attempt to measure the individual policy dimensions. Instead this study measures the extent of the broad policy categories. According to Sapiro, such policies are more important to working women due to the biological differences that "are exaggerated by women's having been given nearly total responsibility for reproduction, child care and even child support" (Sapiro, 1981, p. 704).

Social policy is operationalized here by counting the presence or absence in each country each year of divorce/marriage policy, family/child responsibility policy, domestic violence/rape policy, abortion rights policy, and equality in education policy, all targeting women's needs. The purpose of these five types of policy is to protect the legal, personal, and educational rights of women. The first three of these policies provide legal and financial protection and equality between men and women within the marriage and family structure. Divorce/marriage policy guarantees to the female members of a marriage partnership the same property and parental rights that male members of the partnership have. Family/child responsibility policy provides tax relief, child allowances, and/or housing allowances for families with children to offset the financial burden of family expenditures (Mikkola, 1991). The purpose of domestic violence/rape policy is to protect female members in domestic relationships from abusive behavior that can lead to injury or death. Laws addressing abortion rights limit the state's control over individuals' reproductive freedom. Equal education policies guarantee equal access, opportunity, and treatment for females and males at different educational levels.

According to Marianne Githens (1994) and a wide array of researchers, all of the policies that are used in the operationalization of the dependent variables involve pressing issues that have confronted or are currently confronting women. Although these issues influence the entire population, both directly and indirectly, the issues affect higher numbers of women directly. Conceptualizing these policies as women's interests has support in both theory and previous research.

Two interval scales have been created to represent employment and wage protection policies and social policies for each country. In each case the lack of a policy in a given year is denoted by a 0; as 1 signifies the existence of a policy in a given year. The assigned values for all five policies in each of the two general policy arenas are then summed for each country for each year in the series, producing a low of 0 and a high of 5 in each of the two general policy arenas. Both of the scales range from 0 through 5, with a 0 signifying the lack of any of these particular employment or social policies in a given country in a given year and a 5 exhibiting the existence of all five policies examined in each category. Data for these measures is acquired from the various sources listed in the appendix.

Independent Variables

The principal independent variable for this study is the percentage of women in policy-making positions. Because this is a comparative study dealing with the legislative process of various industrialized nations, the place of policy origin must be considered when examining who is influential in the policy-making process. In most of the included nations, policy mainly originates in the executive branch (Doring, 1995). However, in the United States, policy generally originates in the legislative branch rather than in the executive branch. Therefore, depending on the point of origin for legislation in the country, this variable is operationalized by using the percentage of female cabinet members or the percentage of females in the legislature, whichever is appropriate to the country in question.

Research suggests that the length of time a representative is in office has an impact on influencing policy (Fenno, 1987; Thomas, 1994; Gertzog, 1995), although there is a lack of consensus regarding the length of time in office that is necessary to influence the policy process. Newly elected representatives lack the opportunity and experience to influence policy output. As female officeholders gain seniority, they also acquire committee appointments and gain influence within the committees, resulting in their leadership and increased effectiveness in the policy-making process. Therefore, we presume that female policymakers who are recently elected will have little if any effect on policy making, and we propose that, to be effective, policymakers need to hold office for an undetermined amount of time.

For this study, the percentage of female policymakers variable was run without a lag, with a one-year lag, with a two-year lag, with a three-year lag, and with a four-year lag. When all five measures of the independent variable were included in a regression, the variable with the four-year lag was the only significant variable of the five. Based on this outcome the percentage of female policymakers variable is measured with a four-year lag; this amount of time is expected to be enough for an influence to affect the policy process.[3] The specific hypotheses addressed in this first analysis are:

1. The greater the representation of female policymakers in any country at any time, the greater the likely presence of employment and wage protection policies.

2. The greater the representation of female policymakers in any country at any time, the greater the likely presence of social policies to protect women.

If the number of female policymakers influences the legislative outcome by generating the types of governmental policies mentioned earlier, all other factors being equal, then the independent variable will be significant in the analysis. In this case, the relationship is expected to be significant in a positive direction.

To distinguish the effects of the female representation variables on the dependent variables, controls must be introduced. At a minimum, alternative political actors must be considered: certainly the heads of a nation exert direct influence over policy formulation. Additionally, the fact that the head of government in parliamentary governments chooses the people who make up the executive cabinet demonstrates that the head of government may exert indirect influence in the policy-making process prior to the actual formulation of specific policies. In consideration of this potential influence, a dummy variable is included to distinguish between a male or female head of government, with 0 signifying a male and 1 signifying a female. Based on the theory that women in government are more likely than men to support women's issues, the expectation is that female heads of government will choose cabinet members who will also support women's issues. Therefore, this variable is expected to have a positive influence on both dependent variables.

Another controlled variable is the percentage of Catholics in the population. Research has shown that Catholic nations have not taken the expansion of women's rights as seriously as other nations have, resulting in a delay in the passage and implementation of such rights, including voting and property rights (Sapiro, 1981; Lovenduski, 1986). Catholic nations have also demonstrated a traditional lack of acceptance of female participation in the workforce (Blau & Ferber, 1992), provisions for child care facilities (Norris, 1987), divorce reforms (Norris, 1987), and reproduction policies (Sapiro 1981), resulting in the expectation of a negative relationship between this variable and the dependent variables. Interval-level data representing the percentage of the population that is Catholic is used to measure this variable.[4]

However, contrary to expectation, Catholic nations (except Spain and Ireland) tend to have more liberal abortion laws than many of the Protestant countries do. The explanation for this tendency is that although parties shape the formulation of policies resulting in the establishment of legal rights to abortion, economic and religious factors influence the actual implementation of abortion services. Liberal and socialist parties are influential in the policy-making process of the Catholic nations, resulting in the creation of more liberal abortion laws. However, the national economy and dominant religious affiliation affects the implementation of abortion laws through limited services in hospitals and clinics, noncooperation of medical staff, or conservative social attitudes (Norris, 1987).

As mentioned earlier, the social policy dependent variable is operationalized by the presence or absence of five individual policies, with one of the policies being abortion rights policy. Although the other four policies used in the operationalization of this dependent variable are expected to be negatively influenced by the Catholic variable, the possibility exists that the abortion rights policy may be positively influenced by the Catholic variable, resulting in a flawed measure of the dependent variable. Therefore, two distinct analyses will be conducted using the social policy variable, and a third separate analysis will be performed using the abortion rights policy as a dichotomous variable to isolate the possible positive influence of the Catholic variable. The first analysis will include the abortion rights policy in the measurement of the social policy variable as explained earlier; the second will exclude the abortion rights policy from the measurement of the dependent variable, modifying the summed values to produce a low of 0 and a high of 4; the third analysis will be conducted using a 0 to signify the absence of an abortion rights policy and a 1 to signify the presence of an abortion rights policy.

Based on previous research, variables representing the type of political party controlling the government and the influence of a socialist party in the government are also controlled. Generally, researchers (Hibbs, 1977; Hewitt, 1977; Castles, 1982) suggest that the political party in control has a major influence on the determination of policy making. Parties of the left, center, and right are likely to support significantly different policy agendas. In the United States, Leader (1977) found that although female legislators tend to be more supportive than their male counterparts of women's issue policies, party is still a stronger predictor of policy support.

Looking specifically at socialist parties in the industrialized nations, we find these parties lean toward a more egalitarian ideology and exhibit this by providing female party members with the opportunities to acquire and maintain political office (Norris, 1987). This ideological conviction is expected to emerge in the types of policies that socialist representatives support. Skjeie (1993) observed that the Norwegian Socialist party platform included various family-based care policy proposals. In a more cross-national study, Norris (1987) found that liberal and socialist parties are more likely to initiate and support certain women's issue policies such as abortion rights and child care. However, the findings of other scholars (Parkin, 1971; Jackman, 1980) contradict this research, demonstrating that socialist party strength has very little if any effect on policies addressing equality.

For this study, type of political party is operationalized as an ordinal variable, with conservative given the value of -1, moderate given the value of 0, and liberal given the value of 1. This ordinal-level scale is derived from the classification utilized by

Norris (1987). An interval-level variable shows the percentage of socialists in the government.[5] Both variables are expected to have positive relationships with the dependent variables.

According to Gary Marks (1989), in all Western societies individual unions and groups of unions pursue specific governmental policies for the benefit of their members. These policies include better working conditions, increased wages, advancement opportunities, unemployment benefits, and personal leave security. In return, policymakers rely on unions for voter support, making the relationship advantageous to both. We can deduce that the composition of the unions' membership influences the types of policies that the unions pursue (Cook, 1980; Jonasdóttir, 1988). Therefore, it is possible that as the level of female membership increases, more policies addressing female concerns will be pursued.

Since labor unions are influential in many of the nations included in this study and because one of the dependent variables deals with protecting women's employment and wage rights, it is necessary to include a control for the union influence on policy outcome. Specifically we control for the percentage of female union membership on the expectation that greater female union representation will be associated with policies for equality in wage opportunities and employment. However, the variable is not expected to have an effect on the social policy variable since union activity or support does not directly influence the five individual policies that make up the social policy variable.

A variable for the percentage of women in the labor force is also included in this study as a control for the expected changes in attitudes and behavior associated with an increase in women's employment (Anderson, 1975; Welch, 1977; Gurin, 1987) and their effect on policy outcome. Prior to the growth in female labor, the ideal work for women was to remain in the home, caring for the family; public policy reflected this homebound status. However, as more women took jobs outside the home, these policies needed to be replaced. This resulted in the development of policies targeting female concerns and discrimination against women in the workplace (Githens, 1994).

Besides its effect on equal employment and wage protection policy, the percentage of women in the labor force is also expected to influence the formulation of social policy. As women have gained their economic freedom through expanding employment opportunities, they have found it less necessary to remain in unhappy or abusive marriages. Women are also aware that the decisions they make regarding reproductive freedom and educational advancement will influence their new employment opportunities. Therefore, as women continue to increase their participation in the labor force, we can expect that policies will be formulated to address the issues relating to women's changing social and workplace status.

In addition, the percentage of women in the population of childbearing age, defined as 15 to 44 years old, is controlled for its constituency effect on employment, wage protection policy, and social policy. This is based on the assumption that women in this age group want employment status protection and advancement opportunities while they are starting and raising their families. Women in this age group are also concerned with financial child care issues and reproductive rights since these women are customarily responsible for child care and reproductive choices. All three of these variables use interval-level data obtained from various sources listed in the appendix. All are expected to have positive relationships with the dependent variables.

Some of the nations included in this study have produced equal wage and equal employment policies through the collective bargaining process rather than directly through the legislative process. The practice of collective bargaining is a form of interaction between actors within the industrial relations system, with the main actor being the union or a group of unions. Collective bargaining cannot take place without the presence of a union or unions. The other actors taking part in this relationship are the managers and their hierarchy within the business and in employer associations, and the regulators or agents of the government who are involved in the industrial relations system. Additional actors that may be called into the process as arbitrators are the nongovernmental agents and agencies (Beal et al., 1976).

Because actors other than the national legislators that are examined in this study influence the policies that are formulated through the collective bargaining process, it is necessary to control for this different form of policy making. To do this a dichotomous variable will be included to distinguish if the policies that compose the dependent variables were formulated by collective bargaining or by the legislative process. The policies produced through collective bargaining will be given the value of 1; policies produced through the national legislative process will be given the value of 0.[6] Data for this variable is gathered from the *OECD Employment Outlook*.

Finally, research on the effects of levels of wealth on policy formulation impel us to control for gross domestic product per capita. Studies of various industrialized nations, including the United States and Britain, suggest that economic factors have a profound effect on policy making (Dye, 1976; Jackman, 1980; King, 1981; Rose, 1984), with the level of economic development influencing the issues that legislators choose to target. Examples of resource-influenced policy issues include social security, unemployment, and wealth redistribution; the economic growth of a nation is viewed as a main cause for the emergence of the welfare state (Wilensky, 1975). This variable uses interval-level data[7] and is expected to have a positive relationship with the dependent variables. However, Castles (1982) found that the relationships between gross national product growth and changes in spending on education, income maintenance, and health are in the negative direction.[8]

Methodology

As mentioned earlier this study attempts to further the research addressing female policymakers' influence on policy outcome by taking a more extensive cross-national approach than has previous research and by conceptualizing women's issues as two distinct policy realms. To accomplish this task, it is necessary to use a method of analysis that incorporates the 35-year period and the 22 individual nations of this study. By using pooled time-series analysis, we can combine the two entities in a single study. Another benefit to using this method is that it provides a sufficient number of observations for proper analysis. Rather than limiting the number of observations to 35 or 22 when using time-series or cross-sectional analysis, using the "nation year" as the unit of analysis multiplies the number of observations. The results are presented in chapter five.

THE SECOND ANALYSIS

The second analysis attempts to study the effect of female policy makers on the substance of policy that has been adopted, focusing on the elements that make up a specific women's issue policy rather than on the sheer presence or absence of a variety of policies. Equal wage legislation is the policy selected here for more detailed examination; our concern is whether variation or change in female policy-making representation is reflected in the substance of the policy.

Although there is some argument about what causes the differential between male and female salaries, most researchers agree that a wage differential exists. The literature addressing the inequality of wages confirms that a gender wage gap exists (Cotton, 1988; Heywood & Nezlek, 1993) and is not a new phenomenon. Data from the 1950s reveal significant differentials between male and female salaries throughout the industrialized nations (Blau & Ferber, 1992). However, other researchers find that although there is a wage gap, the gap is declining (O'Neill,

1990; Sorensen, 1991), and the differential varies considerably among the studied nations (Chiplin & Sloane, 1976; Siebert & Sloane, 1980; Miller, 1987).

As a result of these findings, individual nations as well as groups of nations have attempted to curtail wage inequality. Besides including wage equality provisions in individual constitutions and national or subnational legislation, both the International Labor Organization (ILO) and the European Community (EC) established equal remuneration provisions and urged member nations to adopt the provisions. Of those researchers who study the effectiveness of governmental policies and find a declining wage gap, some contend that wage-equalizing policies are instrumental in curtailing the wage disparity (Leijon, 1975; Zabalza & Tzannatos, 1985). Smith and Ward (1984) maintain that governmental policies are not responsible for the changes that have occurred. These dissenters give credit to other societal factors for the declining wage gap.

Further research proposes that the remedy for wage inequality lies in decreased job segregation. Studies focusing on job segregation and its effects suggest that gender wage discrepancies exist because the typical jobs held by women, i.e., "pink collar" jobs, customarily offer lower wages than do those jobs predominantly held by men (Treiman & Terrell, 1975; England & Norris, 1985). Two solutions are offered to solve the wage disparity between male and female workers resulting from job segregation: expanding employment opportunities for women and promoting the comparable worth technique of wage classification. The first solution of expanding employment opportunities relies on the formulation of, and compliance with, effective equal employment opportunity legislation. This type of legislation attacks the discriminatory practices of employers in hiring, promoting, transferring, assigning, and paying employees (Killingsworth, 1990). The second solution suggests comparing the skills, effort, responsibility, and working conditions of jobs predominantly held by women with the same factors in jobs usually held by men (Killingsworth, 1990; England, 1992); these comparisons would be used to classify the wage levels among different yet comparable jobs.

Despite the arguments that equal wage policies are ineffective or that job segregation is the real culprit in maintaining the gender wage disparity, this part of the study suggests that women in general, and female policymakers specifically, believe that equal wage policies are formulated to correct wage disparities. Therefore, this analysis proposes that as we get a greater representation of female policymakers, more effective equal wage policies will be formulated.

This analysis uses a cross-national sample of 18 nations. Because the equal wage policies of four of the nations used in the first analysis (Australia, Belgium, Finland, and Switzerland) were formulated through the collective bargaining process or a separate government commission rather than through the legislative process, or address the equal wage dilemma within the national constitution, these nations will be excluded from this part of the study. However, for the same reasons mentioned in the first analysis, the nations under examination are all industrialized, capitalist democracies and the same time period, 1960 to 1994, is used. Once again this analysis excludes the specific years that Greece, Portugal, and Spain were not considered democracies.

The dependent variable for this part of the study is legislation addressing wage equality and is operationalized by using the equal wage laws of each of the nations. For this research, equal wage laws refer to legislation that prevents employers from discriminating against employees by assigning different wages to them based on their sex even though they are doing the same, similar, or comparable work. Based on past inequalities, we can deduce that laws enacted for the purpose of equalizing the salaries of all workers are important to women since female workers historically have been paid less than male workers.

Two scales have been constructed to measure the substantive elements of the equal wage laws. Both scales provide a measure of the comprehensiveness of the policy. Construction of the first scale considers the goals that are established for each specific law. As the equal wage laws were formulated, general goals were set for each piece of legislation. For the early laws, the main goal was to achieve equal pay for the same, broadly similar, or like job. By requiring that the comparison be made between a man and a women holding the same, broadly similar, or like job, those formulating the legislation greatly limited the field of jobs to which the laws applied; the laws did not address the wage disparities resulting from the high degree of occupational seg-regation found throughout the world (OECD, 1988).

As later laws were formulated, the goal of the laws became equal pay for work of equal value. The concept of work of equal value permits making comparisons between different types of work rather than limiting the comparisons to similar or identical jobs. This notion allows for wages to be compared between em-ployees whose jobs are determined to be of equal value to the employer, thus expanding the types of jobs to which the laws applied. However, the maintenance of all-male and all-female jobs under different employers still hindered the scope of appli-cation of the laws (OECD, 1988).

Recently, a new concept has been proposed as a goal for future laws and is being implemented in a few of the current laws. This concept of equal pay for work of comparable worth emphasizes the comparability of jobs. According to Killingsworth (1990), two jobs are considered of comparable worth when the skills, effort, responsibility, and working conditions of the two jobs are viewed as comparable; this is especially important when the jobs being compared are typically categorized as all-male or all-female jobs. Although defining this concept based on the four factors mentioned above is more difficult than defining the pre-vious two concepts, adoption of this goal would widen the ap-plication of the laws by allowing comparisons to be made between jobs under different employers (OECD, 1988).

It is noticeable that the OECD suggests a progression in the advancement of the laws' goals. This progression is due to the laws' range of application going from same work to work of equal value to comparable work. The first scale has been constructed to measure this progression. The range of the scale is from 0 through 3, with 0 signifying no law, 1 signifying a law of equal pay for equal work, 2 signifying a law of equal pay for work of equal value, and 3 signifying a law of equal pay for comparable work.

The second scale considers to whom the laws apply and which jobs the legislation covers. Application of the laws determines whether they address general wage inequality of both men and women or if they focus on the wage inequality with which female employees struggle. Many of the laws take the general approach and focus on abolishing all forms of wage inequality without emphasizing the sex of the workers. This method stresses the "equality for all" concept. Other laws take the second approach by acknowledging that female workers suffer from the wage differential far more than male workers do. By acknowledging this sex-based wage disparity, the laws attempt to rectify the problem through legislation demanding the equalization of wages between the sexes. This method stresses the concept of "equal wages for women" in relation to the wages that men receive.

Besides considering if the legislation addresses the equality issue in a general manner or if it specifically targets the unequal status of women, it is also important to note if the legislation covers all or only select forms of employment. Although many of the laws require that all jobs comply with the provisions of the laws, upon examination we find that some of the individual laws include exemptions for certain jobs. These exemptions are due to the existence of gender-dominated occupations as well as other forces, such as government or union influence.

In the construction of this scale, it is assumed that laws addressing equality for all men and women are less focused on the female problem of wage inequality and are therefore considered lower on the scale of women's issues. Along this line, laws that target the consistent wage discrepancy by focusing on achieving equal wages for women are considered higher on the scale of women's issues. It is also assumed that laws covering all jobs are more thorough attempts at targeting the equality problem than are laws that exempt certain jobs. Therefore, the values of the scale are as follows: 0 signifies no law, 1 signifies a law focusing on equality for those applying to certain jobs, 2 signifies a law focusing on equality for those applying to all jobs or a law focusing on equal wages for women applying to certain jobs and 3 signifies a law focusing on equal wages for women applying to all jobs. As is noted from this explanation, the range of the scale is from 0 to 3, with 3 measuring the most thorough equal wage laws. All of the data in the construction of the two mentioned scales is gathered from sources listed in the appendix.

Because this analysis addresses the effect that the amount of female policymakers has on policy formulation, it uses the same principal independent variable as the first analysis: percentage of women in policy-making positions. The specific hypothesis addressed in this analysis is:

The greater the representation of female policymakers in any country at any time, the greater the comprehensiveness of governmental policies addressing wage equality.

As in the first analysis, there are other variables that need to be controlled to differentiate the main independent variable's influence on the dependent variable from other factors. As discussed previously in regard to the summary measures of the employment and wage protection policy and the social policy, we expect the gender of the head of government, type of political party controlling the government, percentage of socialists in the government, percentage of female union membership, and percentage of women in the labor force to positively influence the scope of equal wage legislation. It is also expected that the percentage of Catholics in the population will negatively influence the scope of the equal wage legislation. The expectation of a negative influence is due to research (Lovenduski, 1986) suggesting that the Catholic Church has traditionally opposed women's social and political emancipation. In certain nations, the Catholic hierarchy has influenced many areas of education (Inglehart, 1981) and family policy (Caldwell, 1982), resulting in the maintenance of the conservative belief that the woman's place is in the home dominated by the man. Evidence of the negative influence is revealed in the labor force where women in Catholic, European nations are less likely to be employed than women in Protestant, European nations (Blau & Ferber, 1992). Therefore, the smaller percentage of females in the labor force does not provide the incentive to expand the scope of the equal wage policies.

Methodology

This part of the study uses two separate methods of analysis. First, the equal wage laws will be presented in a descriptive analysis with six specific characteristics examined to help determine the content of the individual laws. The characteristics are:

1. problems targeted by the policies,
2. objectives of the policies,
3. enforcement measures included in the policies,
4. commissions established by the policy to control implementation and enforcement,
5. amendments to the original policy,
6. obstacles to the policies.

Rather than analyze each national law individually, the nations are grouped into six categories (one of the categories being Japan) and the policies are examined and compared within these groups. The categorization of the nations will be based on cultural, historical, religious, labor force, and/or regional similarities. Previous research (Lovenduski, 1986; Kaplan, 1992) has indicated that many policies show distinct similarities tied to common cultural, historical, or regional features. Analysis of the equal wage policies of individual nations here showed a similar pattern and are thus grouped as follows: the North American nations, the Commonwealth and former Commonwealth nations excluding Canada, the Mediterranean nations, the Scandinavian nations, the remainder of the European nations, and Japan. A descriptive analysis will illustrate the relevant policy commonalties as well as their cultural, historical, and regional correlates.

Following the descriptive analysis, a pooled quantitative analysis will be conducted using the two dependent variables and the independent variables mentioned previously.

NOTES

1. The countries included in this study are Australia, Austria, Belgium, Canada, Denmark, Finland, France, Germany, Greece, Iceland, Ireland, Italy, Japan, the Netherlands, New Zealand, Norway, Portugal, Spain, Sweden, Switzerland, the United Kingdom and the United States.

2. Researchers discussing "women's policies" or "interests" are often examining very different things (from equality with men to special needs involving family responsibilities). Hence, studies and results aren't really comparable.

3. Sources used for this data include *The European Journal of Political Research* vol. 22, no. 4, *The World's Women 1970–1990 Trends and Statistics* (United Nations, 1991) and *The Political Handbook of the World* (various volumes).

4. This data is obtained from the *Political Data Handbook* and *World Christian Encyclopedia*.

5. Data for these variables are found in the *Political Data Handbook* and *Political Parties in Western Democracies*.

6. Data for this variable is gathered from the *OECD Employment Outlook*.

7. Data for this variable is found in *OECD National Accounts, OECD Main Economic Indicators*, and the *United Nations Statistical Yearbook* (various years).

8. Only the relationship between Gross National Product (GNP) growth and changes in spending on education is statistically significant at the .05 level.

Comparing Equal Wage Policies

NORTH AMERICAN NATIONS

The United States and Canada make up this category. Both of these countries share many similarities, making the decision to analyze the two together a logical one. These similarities include both countries being federal democracies, neither having a dominant national religion, both having multicultural populations resulting from waves of immigration, and both having separate, specific powers assigned to the state and provincial governments. Besides these similarities, the two nations share a vast border. Due to this shared border, it is likely that situations occurring in either of these countries, such as the formation of popular movements, mass demonstrations, or policy developments, will influence conditions in the other country.

Although equal wage policies in the United States have been in operation at the state level since 1919, the 1963 Equal Pay Act was the first piece of federal legislation prohibiting sex discrimination to be passed. Prior to this, separate wage scales could be maintained for female and male workers doing identical jobs for the same employer. At the time of its passage, women were being paid 60 percent of what the average man was being paid (Greenberger, 1980).

Originally, the act included equal pay for comparable work; however, following congressional debate, the wording changed to equal pay for equal work. Although the definition of equal work is problematic due to the vagueness of the wording, the courts have broadened the definition of the word "equal" from "identical" to "substantially equal" for the purpose of including jobs that are performed under similar working environments and require equal effort, skill, and responsibility (Williams & Bagby, 1984). The stated purpose of the act was to "prohibit discrimination on account of sex," and although the wording did not specify that women should be paid the same as men, it is assumed from knowledge of the existing wage differential that women were the ones who benefited from this policy.

Besides the vagueness of the phrase "equal work," another problem with the original legislation was that 11 categories of employment[1] were exempted from coverage. In an effort to expand the application of the law in the workforce, it was amended in 1972 by the Education Amendments Act. This revision expanded the field of jobs that must comply with the law to include employees holding executive, administrative, and professional positions, as well as outside salespersonnel. Further changes in 1974 brought additional employees under the protection of the law, including most federal, state, and local government workers (Greenberger, 1980).

Enforcement of the act is one of the responsibilities of the Equal Employment Opportunity Commission (EEOC). Those who believe they have a case against an employer for noncompliance with the law can sue the employer. However, one shortcoming of the law is that class action suits may not be brought. The burden of proof for court cases addressing violations of the law is left up to the plaintiffs, who must show that although the work is largely the same based on the above mentioned requirements, the women are paid less than the men. There are justifications included in the law for wage differentials for equal work. These justifications include seniority, merit, and payment based on quality or quantity of production or factors other than sex (England, 1992).

In Canada, provincial laws enforcing equal wages for women have been around since 1951 but not at the national level. Due to the individual requirements of each province, wording for the laws varied slightly, with the main approach being the requirement of equal pay for both men and women when they work at the same establishment and perform jobs that are identical (Marsden, 1980). Even with the provincial laws, the 1961 Canadian census revealed a female to male wage differential of .54 for all workers and .59 for full-year workers (Gunderson, 1975).

In 1971, equal pay provisions were included in the federal Canadian Labour Code to address discrimination against both men and women. The wording for this code modified the definition of job requirements to include employment "under the same or similar working conditions, the same or similar work on jobs requiring the same or similar skill, effort and responsibility" (Marsden, 1980). Since labor legislation is under provincial jurisdiction, the federal legislation influences only specific interprovincial or international industries such as interprovincial transportation, communication, air transport, broadcasting, shipping, and banking (Gunderson, 1975).

Despite the initial provincial attempts at documenting wage equality for women and men and the 1971 rewording to expand the description of what jobs deserved equal compensation, wage inequalities remained due to persistent job segregation. These "job ghettos" made the existing equal wage legislation impractical. The only possible solution to the wage inequality problem was for Canada to make a commitment to the International Labor Organization (ILO) Convention 100, calling for the further redefinition of equal wage legislation by requiring "equal pay for work of equal value" or comparable worth. The ILO Convention had been ratified by Canada, but implementation had not taken place (Marsden, 1980).

Efforts were made on the parts of Canadian women's organizations, members of Parliament, political parties, and government officials in the Ministry of Labour to urge the implementation of the principles behind the ILO Convention 100. Rather than redress the original provisions included in the Canadian Labour Code, Bill C–25, also known as the Canadian

Human Rights Act, was introduced and passed by the federal legislature in 1977 to address the equal value debate. Under the act, the value of jobs is dependent on the effort, responsibility, and skill that is required to perform the job. Workers performing equal value jobs must also be employed by the same employer for the jobs to be considered equal. A wage difference would be justified if the difference is due to another "reasonable factor" such as seniority. The enforcement of the act is left to the Human Rights Commission, which was established to handle the complaints of noncompliance with the Act (Marsden, 1980).

Although the passage of the Human Rights Act instituted the formal rewording of equal pay for work of equal value, supporters of the principle of equality were not fully satisfied. Those involved in the debate had hoped that the new definition would be made to the Canadian Labour Code since human rights laws lack the constitutional basis to protect them from other legislation. Instead supporters had to settle for implementation of the new concept in a less protected format (Marsden, 1980).

COMMONWEALTH AND FORMER COMMONWEALTH NATIONS (EXCLUDING CANADA)

In this category we examine the policies of Britain, Ireland, and New Zealand. These three nations are examined together primarily due to their past and present Commonwealth link. The history and culture of Britain (the power behind the Commonwealth) have been strongly influential in the development of the Irish and New Zealand nations. (Though Canada has also been influenced by British history and culture, the country has a significant link to French history and culture and therefore is excluded from this category.) Although these three nations are not located in one region, their shared Commonwealth past and current relationship is useful in explaining similarities found in their governments and societies. We find that the governments in Ireland and New Zealand were fashioned after the British parliamentary system and British immigration has contributed in both positive and negative ways to the cultures of Irish and New Zealand societies.

It is important to note the religious difference among the three nations that has shown to be influential. Because Protestant religions are dominant in Britain and New Zealand and the Catholic religion is dominant in Ireland, it is not improbable to expect some policy-making differences due to religious conviction. The Catholic Church is recognized for being less supportive of women's rights when those rights are counter to religious doctrine. Catholic opposition in policy formulation has been evident in regard to such matters as divorce, contraception, and abortion rights policies. However, the historical link is evident in the three nations' maintenance of strong trade and cultural ties.

Since Britain is the common link among these nations, we will begin with the British case. During the 1970s, legislation was introduced in Britain to address the inequalities between male and female employment. Prior to the legislation, women earned approximately 58 percent of what men earned (OECD, 1988). The Equal Pay Act of 1970 was designed to require equal pay for female and male workers who are employed by the same employer and perform the same or relatively similar work. The policy was intended to apply to all forms of employment, including full-time and part-time. Enforcement of the 1970 act was left in the hands of industrial tribunals and the Central Arbitration Committee. When the act was passed in 1970, employers were permitted to take five years to implement the requirements of the legislation, weakening the immediate influence of the policy (MacLennan & Fonda, 1985).

Although the act specifies that it applies to all employment, this is deceptive. To evaluate the equivalence of the jobs, a job rating system was created. Unfortunately the practice of evaluating the same or similar jobs held by both men and women working for the same employer runs into difficulties due to the frequent problem of job segregation. Certain jobs are primarily held by men, and other jobs are primarily held by women. For cases of noncompliance, the act allows equal wage claims to be pursued only when individuals compare their work with the work of someone of the opposite sex. If women work only or primarily with other women, equal pay tends to be a nonissue (Collins, 1992).

In 1983, an amendment was introduced to the Equal Pay Act. The amendment, which took effect in 1984 and was implemented by the British government to conform to demands by the European Commission, expanded the types of jobs that can be considered in an equal wage claim. The amendment made it possible for the Equal Pay Act to apply to women working in traditionally female-held jobs such as those of secretary, receptionist, and canteen staff. Female workers were no longer required to compare their work with the same work of male colleagues. Equal pay for work of equal value based on the effort, skills, and decision making necessary for the job became the requirement. Jobs no longer needed to be considered the "same or broadly similar" and job evaluation studies were no longer required (Collins, 1992).

Similar to their British neighbors, Irish policymakers introduced legislation conforming to the EC directives, targeting pay and employment inequality since at the time, Irish women were earning 56 percent of what Irish men earned (OECD, 1988). The policy took the form of the Anti-Discrimination Act of 1974 (although the act actually became effective in January 1976) and applies to all employment. According to the act, women who are employed by the same or associated employer as their male counterparts are guaranteed the same pay for "like" work. Therefore, the jobs under comparison need not be exactly the same but must be similar (Murdoch, 1984).

To deal with cases of noncompliance, all disputes are directed to an Equality Officer in the Department of Labour. Besides directing disputes to this office, the act also provides remedies and sanctions, such as nondiscrimination notices for noncompliance with the legislation (Murphy, 1993).

As a result of the implementation of the second EC Equal Treatment Directive, the Irish Employment Equality Agency was established in 1977 in association with the Employment Equality Act. Besides reviewing the work of the Employment Equality Act, the agency was given responsibility for policy oversight of the Anti-Discrimination Act and can make recommendations for amendments to the act. The agency is also responsible for investigating complaints of noncompliance and initiating proceedings in cases of discrimination (Murdoch, 1984).

On the other side of the globe we find New Zealand. It would appear that the preliminary equal wage policy in New Zealand was the 1960 Government Service Equal Pay Act. However, this policy only applied to government workers, excluding all private-sector employees. In actuality the first policy to thoroughly address the wage discrepancy between men and women in the country was the 1972 Equal Pay Bill. Prior to the passage of the bill, women were earning approximately 71 percent of the average male weekly earnings (Nieuwenhuysen & Hicks, 1975). The bill proposed the elimination of pay discrimination for men and women in the same or broadly similar employment that required the same or similar skills, effort, and responsibility. Application of the bill was to include all jobs, including female-intensive industries (Haines, 1992). The bill also provided a "phasing in" period to be completed by 1977. The Court of Arbitration was given authority to require compliance by all parties involved with the policy (Nieuwenhuysen & Hicks, 1975). Despite the bill's application to all jobs and its appearance of attacking wage discrimination against all women in the labor force, the legislation is far from effective. The bill addresses the equal pay for equal work concept rather than expanding the legislation to cover work of equal value. By limiting the comparability of the jobs, the bill justifies the wage differentials. Furthermore, the implementation and enforcement of the New Zealand bill was not an immediate process since the bill allowed the five-year phasing-in period for employers.

MEDITERRANEAN NATIONS

The four countries included in this category not only share regional (southern Europe) and religious (primarily Catholic) similarities, all four of them have progressed from dictatorial rule to democracy in the past century, three of them since the 1970s. Perhaps due to their relatively recent democratization, Spain, Portugal, Greece, and Italy have struggled politically and economically (Italy has become more economically similar to the other European nations), and their struggles have influenced their view and acceptance of sexual equality. Although the constitutions of all four nations contain articles guaranteeing equality for all citizens, the women in these nations gained the right to vote and hold office later than the women in most of the other industrialized nations.

For no specific reason, this category will begin with an analysis of the Spanish case. With the country's return to democratic rule after the death of Franco, a new constitution was written in 1978. Within the contents of the constitution an attempt was made to enumerate general rights of individuals, including the appearance of equality between the sexes. The Spanish constitution declares that all "Spaniards are equal before the law" regardless of the person's sex, and all citizens have the right to work, choose a profession, be considered for promotion, and receive sufficient remuneration without the threat of sexual discrimination. Article 28 of the new Statute of Workers, which passed in 1980, declared that all employers have the obligation to pay equal wages for equal work. Although this law drew attention to the economic status of women in Spain, its actual effect on wage equality was limited (Flanz, 1983). Women continued to earn approximately 70 percent of what men were earning (Blomquist, 1996).

In 1988, to comply with the European Community Directive 75/117/EEC, which established the principle of equal pay for work of equal value, Spain passed its own Equal Pay Law (Collins, 1992). The purpose of Law 8 was to define discriminatory practices against women, specifically in attaining employment and within the working environment. Law 8 was intended to apply to all forms of employment. The law also prescribes large fines for noncompliance with its principles (Fernandez, 1993).

As in the Spanish Constitution, the Portuguese Constitution, ratified in 1976, includes an article (Article 13) providing equality of rights among citizens. The same article also prohibits discrimination based on many factors, including sex. This general attempt at providing equality for all citizens may appear to prohibit all forms of discrimination; however, the creators of the constitution excluded a provision that specifically addressed the inequality between men and women (Flanz, 1983).

Three years later, with women continuing to earn approximately 76 percent of what men earned (OECD 1988), the 1979 Act on Equality in Work and Employment was formulated to guarantee equal job opportunities and equal treatment at work. Because there is no separate law that deals specifically with the wage equality issue, the issue falls under the subject of equal treatment at work (Carmo Nunes, 1984).

In the Portuguese case, determining wage levels is based on the principle of equal wages for equal work or work of equal value for the same employer. Any variations in pay are justified only if the variations are based on objective criteria and applied to both male and female workers. However, the act does not apply to household employment, other jobs performed in individual homes, or civil servant and local government employment (Carmo Nunes, 1984).

The responsibility for the enforcement of the act is with the Equal Work and Employment Commission, which was established for this purpose. Besides enforcing the act, the commission can also recommend that the Minister of Labour adopt measures to enforce equal opportunities, give advice on cases, and publicize the law. Legal action can be taken by individuals or through labor unions. Workers who feel that they have been discriminated against can take their cases to court without the fear of being fired or punished (Carmo Nunes, 1984).

As in the Spanish and Portuguese documents, the 1975 Greek Constitution guarantees equality, including wage equality, for both men and women. Article 22–1b states that "all workers, irrespective of sex or any other distinction, are entitled to equal remuneration for work of equal value." The provisions established in the constitution prevailed over other legislative provisions opposing the principle of equality (Moussourou & Spiliotopoulos, 1984). However, with the admission of Greece into the EC in 1981 and with the country's compliance with EC law, additional legislation has been designed to further the progress toward wage equality (Collins, 1992).

As of 1984, Greek women were being paid approximately 73 percent of what Greek men were being paid (International Labor Organization). That year, Law 1414 was enacted through the Ministry of Labor to prohibit all types of sexual discrimination with respect to working conditions. This includes inequality of wages. The Equal Pay Directive, incorporated into Law 1414, reinforces the Greek Constitution's commitment of equal pay for work of equal value for women (Miliori, 1993). The law applies to jobs where the conditions of employment are regulated by private law. Therefore, civil service jobs are not subject to the law's regulations (Women of Europe, 1983–1984).

Noncooperation with the law can be dealt with through legal action. However, legal judgments have been limited due to the difficulties of enforcing the equality principles. These problems are due to continual discrimination in arbitration decisions and collective work contracts, hesitancy to take the complaint to court or proceed with court action based on the rules of the directive, and fear of reprisals from employers (Miliori, 1993).

As presented in the studies of the other Mediterranean nations, the Italian Constitution included a guarantee of equality for all citizens. Article 37 sanctions equal pay for equal work. The reality of the situation was that female workers lacked the same opportunities and compensation as their male counterparts did. Even the trade unions, known for their orientation toward defending the interests of those lacking influence, including the female portion of the labor force, categorized female and male workers in different job categories. Men were viewed as the true breadwinners while women were expected to care for the family. Due to this differentiation, the practice of equal pay was not implemented (Beccalli, 1985).

As a result of popular and industrial actions during the 1960s, the achievement of equal pay for equal work was made a reality through the collective bargaining process. The collective agreements successfully reduced the wage differential between men and women by approximately 15 percent (Beccalli, 1985). However, the agreements still did not address the established job segregation that maintained the structural inequality problem, which was viewed as a problem, common to all workers, male and female alike. Therefore, the wage inequality that resulted from job segregation continued (Beccalli, 1985).

In 1977, Law 903, the Equal Treatment in Employment Law, which is not credited to union influence, was passed for the purpose of combating sex discrimination in employment opportunities and treatment. At the time of the law's passage, women were still earning approximately 79 percent of the average male wage (OECD, 1988). According to Article 2 of the law, all female workers deserve the same wages as male workers when they perform jobs that are equal or considered of equal value. This applies to all systems of job classification (Flanz, 1983). According to this law, classifying jobs as either male or female work is prohibited.

Only individual employees can file complaints of noncompliance preventing any type of class action. The burden of proof, in which the standards are not clear, is the responsibility of the individual employee. According to the law, a small fine can be imposed on employers who fail to observe the requirements of Article 2. However, the law does not require that an employer found guilty of discrimination perform any type of compensatory action or provide back pay to the complainant (Beccalli, 1985).

Besides the unclear standards of proving discrimination and the limitation of who can file a complaint, women tend to be unaware of their legal rights (Beccalli, 1985). Therefore, few cases have been filed applying the law. Another reason for the low rate of litigation may be the lack of an oversight committee associated with the law. Although the National Commission for Equal Opportunities now exists to oversee the law, it was not established until 1983, six years after the enactment of the law (Beccalli, 1985). The commission acts in an advisory and investigatory manner in cases of discrimination. Due to its limited powers, the commission does not provide assistance to individuals or become directly involved in cases (Ballestrero, 1984).

SCANDINAVIAN NATIONS

From the southern European countries we go to the northern European countries. This category includes Sweden, Iceland, Norway, and Denmark, otherwise known as the Scandinavian nations. This group of four nations shares many characteristics and are therefore consistently analyzed as a group (Haavio-Mannila et al., 1985; Kaplan, 1992; Karvonen & Selle, 1995). These similar characteristics have been used to explain similar policy developments that have occurred in the four nations.

Besides the obvious similarities of shared regional location and religious affiliation (primarily Protestant), all four democracies are committed welfare states and maintain multiparty, parliamentary systems. Due to these characteristics, we find similar conditions within the four nations that are favorable to their female citizens. Scandinavian women were part of the labor force earlier and at greater numbers than many of their European sisters were. These women also gained the right to vote and hold office earlier (Sweden being the last in 1921) and we find the Scandinavian nations tend to have the largest percentages of female representatives, possibly due to their early labor force involvement and political opportunities.

This category will begin with Sweden. Unlike a number of the previously studied nations, the guarantee of equal treatment for women and men in Sweden is not established in a constitution. For over 40 years the Social Democratic Party and Swedish unions believed themselves to be the best supervisors of workplace equality and therefore were careful about letting government commissions and legislation make decisions about equal opportunity and treatment in employment. Collective bargaining was also viewed as a more flexible method of dealing with changeable workplace conditions. However, in 1976, the new Swedish government elected to formulate legislation addressing the equality issue since women were still earning 85 percent of what men earned (Cook, 1980).

Four years later in 1980, the Swedish Act on Equality Between Men and Women at Work became law, with the purpose of promoting equal rights in employment, working conditions, and opportunities for development. The act provides rules governing sanctions that prohibit discriminatory practices based on sex in both the public and private sectors. Although the act does not specifically address the equal wage issue, prohibiting discrimination in employment can be interpreted as applying to the issue. Section 4 states that employers cannot discriminate on the grounds of sex regarding the terms of employment. This applies to all "like" or equivalent employment. It also offers suggestions for active measures that employers can utilize to promote equality (Flanz, 1983).

To maintain enforcement of the act, the government appointed an Equal Opportunities Ombudsman and an Equal Opportunities Commission to monitor employers' compliance (Ericsson, 1985). Individuals or groups of individuals can take cases of noncompliance to Labour Court or the appropriate district court. Employers who are found to be in noncompliance with the act may be subject to fines or financial restitution (Flanz, 1983).

The act's success in improving conditions for women is not substantial. Affirmative action is not part of the Swedish law due to the lack of an established timetable for compliance with the act and the limited power of the ombudsman to impose compliance by overriding collective agreements. Also, the 1992 amendment to the act refocuses the target of inequality so as to not specifically favor women (Kelber, 1994).

Although we find that the first Equal Pay Act in Iceland came about in 1961 when women were paid about 60 percent of what men were paid (Equal Status Council of Iceland, 1992), the law that is credited for addressing the wage equality issue is the 1976 Law on the Equality of Women and Men. The law not only provides for equal opportunity in employment and education, it also requires that both men and women "receive equal wages for performing comparable work of equal value" for all forms of employment (Flanz, 1983).

The Equality of Treatment Board is responsible for the application and enforcement of the law. For matters of noncompliance, the Board is empowered to bring litigation against violators. Those who are proven to be in violation of the law's provisions are subject to fines unless a heavier penalty is provided by the Board (Flanz, 1983).

One problem with the law deals with the litigation process. Cases that are brought before a court of law are usually costly, lengthy, and complicated, adding to the complainant's dilemma (Haavio-Mannila et al., 1985). Job segregation is also a continuing problem that affects the application of the law's provisions.

In Norway the equal wage issue is contained in the 1978 Act on Equal Status Between the Sexes, which was implemented in 1979. At that time women were earning approximately 80 percent of the average male wage (OECD, 1988). Besides being gender neutral and promoting "equal status between the sexes," the act includes the guarantee of equal pay for work of equal value for men and women who are employed by the same employer. Although it appears that the act applies to all employment sectors, a clause within the policy specifies that the King may prescribe which jobs in central and local government service the act covers (Flanz, 1983).

Enforcement of the Act is delegated to three authorities: the Equal Status Commissioner, or Ombud, addresses allegations of wrong doing from both individuals and groups and pursues voluntary settlements, the Equal Status Appeals Board imposes bans and requirements that are to be implemented, and the Courts of Justice determine judgments on the cases submitted. Even with the oversight of the three authorities, there are problems associated with the enforcement of the law. In many cases it is difficult to produce evidence of discrimination that can be presented in court, and even if pertinent evidence can be found, enforcing the rules is generally a difficult task (Eduards et al., 1985).

Besides these problems, the Norwegian act has its share of critics. Opponents claim that the act promotes sexual equality in general rather than focusing on the inequality suffered specifically by women. Wording of the law is a cause for criticism. With consistent sex segregation in employment, male and female wages cannot be compared unless, as the act specifies, the employees work for the same employer. This provision helps to maintain wage disparities between women and men. In addition, the trade unions in Norway are concerned with the act's inclusion of the equal wage issue. The unions worry that the provisions of the act will intrude on the unions' influence on the rights of free negotiation within employment (Eduards et al., 1985).

Prior to the 1970s in Denmark, there was little legislation that challenged the inequalities between men and women. Women were earning less than 75 percent of what men were earning (Kelber, 1994). Previous social legislation targeted health insurance and poverty. The decade of the 1970s, however, found a great deal of attention focused on the inequalities in society and the workplace. One of the actions taken in 1975 was the establishment of the Equal Status Council, which worked toward the elimination of sexual inequalities in employment (Kelber, 1994).

Unlike the other Scandinavian nations, Danish policy toward the equal wage issue is not incorporated within a general equal status policy but is addressed in a separate, specific policy. In compliance with the EC Equal Pay Directive, the Danish government enacted the 1976 Equal Remuneration Act with the purpose of guaranteeing equal pay to both men and women for the same work in the same workplace. The act allows employees who experience wage discrimination to pursue their case in court and claim compensation from the employer if the employee is dismissed from the job due to the complaint (Flanz, 1983).

There are limitations to the Equal Remuneration Act. The act is limited to achieving equal wages for equal work rather than expanding the definition to include work of comparable worth, placing a limitation on the types of jobs that must comply with the act. Also, the act is only applicable in jobs where collective agreements between employers and unions regarding equal pay are nonexistent (Eduards et al., 1985).

OTHER EUROPEAN NATIONS

The remaining four European nations, Germany, Austria, France, and the Netherlands, are included in this category. All four of the democracies have parliamentary systems, are located in the same geographical region, and share a past that was strongly affected by World War II. The tradition of the four welfare-oriented states is strongly conservative, although France and the Netherlands have an equally strong radical tendency. The persistent male domination in these countries has resulted in government actions that are viewed as nonresponsive—to women's demands (Kaplan, 1992).

In the German case, equality between men and women is not only established by the 1949 Constitution (as well as by the former East German Constitution) but is also declared in the separate lander constitutions. Since the 1940s, the German government has recognized the importance of acknowledging that all people deserve equal rights even though the effort may be purely symbolic. According to Article 3 of the Basic Law, "men and women shall have equal rights" including the right to equal pay. However, the powers of the law are limited due to freedom of contract precedence, which contributes to job segregation and the resulting pay differentials (Schopp-Schilling, 1985), and because of the lack of an established enforcement mechanism included in the legislation. In the past, cases of noncompliance were taken before the labor courts by the individual complainants (Addison, 1975).

Even though the constitution includes the commitment of wage equality between the sexes, actual wage equality was far from a reality, with women earning 72 percent of what their male counterparts earned in the 1970s (Schopp-Schilling, 1985). As Germany moved toward more integration in the European Community, the country took steps to conform with the EC principle of equal wage for work of equal value. In 1980, the German Labour Law was reformed to comply with the EC Directive and, under strong pressure from the EC, the Law Concerning Equal Treatment of Men and Women passed. The new law applies the EC principle to all female and male workers in all sectors of employment (Schopp-Schilling, 1985).

In cases of discrimination, legal action has been sought in the German courts and compensation from employers has been granted. However, the responsibility falls on the employee to provide credible evidence of sexual discrimination. If evidence is produced, the employer must try to demonstrate that the wage discrepancy is justified to avoid a judgment of discrimination (Schopp-Schilling, 1985).

Although the revision of the original statute appears to be in compliance with the EC's equal wage principles, there have been questions regarding the German government's dedication to comply with all of the EC regulations concerning full compensation and sanctions (Schopp-Schilling, 1985). Moreover, four years after the passage of the law, the EC Court of Justice criticized the law for its insufficient enforcement provisions, for which the Ministry of Labour and Social Affairs is responsible (Lemke, 1994).

Even though Austria has one of the highest rates (in the non-communist European nations) of female participation in the labor force, the nation's commitment to equal wages has been modest. In 1958, the principle of equal pay was introduced into the Austrian Constitution under the auspices of human rights. However, there were no enforcement measures developed to deal with noncompliance (Ratner, 1980). Women continued to earn 30 to 40 percent less than men did (OECD, 1988).

It was not until 1979 that actual federal legislation addressing the issue of equal pay was implemented. The legislation came in the form of the Equal Treatment Law. This law imposed a "blanket ban" on all forms of sex discrimination in work relations, including the determination of wages (Flanz, 1983), and granted equal pay for women and men in work of equal value (Kaplan, 1992).

Claims of noncompliance with the law are under the jurisdiction of the Equal Treatment Commission, attached to the Federal Ministry for Social Administration. The commission is responsible for determining the existence or extent of employer discrimination and recommending remedies. If actions are not taken by the employer to terminate the discrimination against the employee, litigation can be pursued in a labor court (Flanz, 1983)

Despite the claim that no one may be discriminated against, the law has its limitations. The law does not apply to all employment. Provisions of the law apply to employment contracts under private law. Therefore, agricultural and forestry workers as well as civil servants are excluded from the law's provisions. The law also lacks significant means of enforcement to discourage future acts of discrimination (Flanz, 1983).

France has a history of recognizing the wage disparity between the sexes. Since the early 1900s, the government, on its own and in compliance with the ILO and Treaty of Rome provisions for equal remuneration for men and women, has made an effort to bring the level of female wages closer to the level of male wages. Even the French Constitutions of 1946 and 1958 promise legal equality between women and men. The main problem with all of these efforts is their lack of sanctions for noncompliance (Stetson, 1987).

In 1971, an advisory group recommended the enactment of an equal pay law with sanctions since the percentage of women in the labor force was increasing but women were earning approximately 66 percent of what men earned (Ratner, 1980). The law,

Act 72–1143 on Equal Remuneration for Men and Women, required equal pay for "the same work or for work of equal value." Act 72–1143 was passed in 1972 and was reaffirmed in 1975 with its compliance to the EC Directive on equal remuneration (Stetson, 1987).

The principle of the law applied to all sectors of the labor market even though it had limited enforcement. Provisions of the law established that the pay rate for women be determined by the same measuring unit used to determine the pay rate for men. This meant that pay rates for both women and men were based on job classification rather than on individual performance (Loree, 1980). With continuing sex segregation in France, whereby females are trapped in the lower-status jobs, the method of using job classification to determine pay levels hinders the reduction of the pay disparity between male and female workers.

The Ministry of Labour is in charge of overseeing the enforcement of the law. Labor inspectors and investigators are responsible for handling complaints and enforcing the law's provisions. Legal action is taken when complaints appear justified. In cases of noncompliance, violators are subject to strict fines (Loree, 1980).

Although the law was a legislative attempt at equalizing wages, the effect of the law was questionable. The intricacies of the wage structure and the absence of a clear definition of "work of equal value" contributed to the difficulties in deciding the success of the law. As a result of these problems and the more general problem of sexual inequality in France, a more comprehensive law, commonly known as the "Roudy Law," was passed in 1983. Although the purpose of the law was to end all forms of sex discrimination and inequality of opportunity in employment, the law also provided a definition of "work of equal value," encompassing the comparison of occupational knowledge, abilities, responsibilities, and physical or mental burdens. Furthermore, the 1983 law required a reexamination by employers of job and salary classification (Stetson, 1987).

High levels of sex segregation in employment is a dilemma

the Netherlands shares with most of the other nations in this study. Due to sex segregation and other problems confronting the Dutch women, including an exemption clause in the nation's Minimum Wage Law that allows employers to pay less than minimum wage to part-time workers (who are usually women), the 1975 Equal Pay Law has not had a large amount of success in its attempt to equalize wages. The law mandates equal pay for equal work or work of equal value for female employees in all full-time positions. Due to the country's Minimum Wage Law, provisions of the Equal Pay Law do not apply to certain part-time employment (Asscher-Vonk, 1995). At the time of its passage, women earned almost 80 percent of what men earned. That percentage has decreased in the years following the passage of the law (OECD, 1988).

In circumstances of possible discrimination, the law allows individuals, not groups, to file complaints to the Equal Pay Law Committee. If the complaint is justified, the committee requests additional information from the employer. Therefore, employees that file complaints may not remain anonymous in the process (de Rijik, 1984).

In those cases where wage discrimination charges are considered valid, employers are required to pay the differences in wages. However, the law does not impose fines or require payment for damages. The only other useful sanction that can be gained from legal cases brought against employers is the resulting publicity. Due to the limitation in the type of punishment that can be dispensed, the law is not considered to be effective (de Rijik, 1984).

Besides the absence of severe sanctions applied to those who do not comply with the law, the classification system of employment contributes to the preservation of the divisions between female and male work. As a result of these divisions it is difficult to prove that certain female jobs are comparable to male jobs. Thus, female jobs are considered on a lower level than male jobs and therefore pay less (de Rijik, 1984).

In 1984, a revision was made to incorporate the Equal Pay

Act and the existing Equal Treatment Act into one policy. However, this revision did not change the objective of the previous equal pay policy (Asscher-Vonk, 1995).

JAPAN

The final nation to be analyzed here is Japan. For this study, Japan constitutes its own category due to its regional location (isolated from the other industrialized democracies) and the specific characteristics that the country does not share with the other industrialized nations. These characteristics include historical, cultural, and religious differences that influence the country's view of government and society. The resulting traditional viewpoint manifests itself in the country's decision and policy making. Japanese policies have attempted to protect women rather than guarantee their equality with men. As a result, women in Japan gained the right to vote relatively late (1945) compared to many of the other democracies in this study. Besides the vote, female participation in the labor force and in government is at a lower level than in most of the other included nations, contributing to the maintenance of the male-dominated society.

However, along with the other industrialized democracies, Japan has taken preliminary steps to work for equality among its citizens. The initial attempt can be found in the nation's constitution. As we find in many of the previously mentioned countries, the Japanese Constitution provides for equality under the law. Article 14 of the constitution states that all people are equal and discrimination based on race, creed, social status, family origin, or sex is prohibited in economic, political, and social relations. The Labor Standards Act of 1947, Article 4, reinforces the constitution's promotion of equality by guaranteeing equal wages for equal work for both sexes, applying to all employment. The purpose of this law was not to promote equality but to improve the economic and social status of Japanese female workers, who were customarily considered inferior to male workers, through protective measures. Those in violation of the act were subject to fines or prison sentences not exceeding six months (Hayashi, 1985).

The act provided for a network of inspectors from the Central Labor Standards Bureau and District Labor Standards Offices to enforce the provisions. Individual workers who question employer compliance with the act can request inspections. In addition, the Women's and Minors' Bureau of the Ministry of Labor works with the inspectors to further interpret and investigate claims of noncompliance (Takahashi, 1976).

Unfortunately women continued to earn approximately 53 percent of what men earned (Yoko et al., 1994). Responsibility for the continued wage disparity was blamed on the vagueness of the expression, "equal wages for equal work," and on the persistent sex segregation throughout the country. The guarantee of equal pay for equal work is difficult to enforce due to the problem of determining what constitutes equal work. The expression also limits the types of jobs that can be compared since women in Japan seldom hold the same jobs as men due to the traditional values that limit the types of jobs women are able to obtain. Since sex discrimination in other areas of employment besides wages is not explicitly prohibited, women are unable to acquire the higher-paying, secure jobs that men monopolize. Women's jobs tend to be part-time, temporary, expendable, and therefore poorly paid. The comparable worth issue has not been discussed in Japan since specifying and defining the comparable worth of male and female jobs is a difficult task (Iwao, 1993).

A more recent legislative attempt was made in 1972 to promote and improve the status of working women, including the issue of equal wages, by prohibiting discriminatory treatment on the basis of sex. Enforcement of the Working Women's Welfare Act is the responsibility of the Women's and Minors' Bureau. However, the act lacks a penalty clause, causing it to have very little influence on those it regulates (Hayashi, 1985).

OVERVIEW

Although the 18 nations included in this part of the study are analyzed by grouping them together based on cultural, historical, and regional commonalties, similar policy characteristics are also apparent. In the two North American nations, we find subnational legislation targeting wage inequality prior to the formulation of national legislation. Initially the purpose of both national policies was equal pay for equal or same work for both sexes. However, in compliance with the ILO Directive, the Canadian policy was amended to include equal pay for work of equal value. We also find that, initially, both policies did not cover certain types of employment, although the U.S. policy has expanded its job coverage over the years.

By analyzing Britain, Ireland, and New Zealand together, we notice that all three countries produced national-level equal wage laws in the 1970s that allowed for phasing-in periods ranging from two to five years. When the policies were implemented, the goal of each was to require equal pay for same or similar work; however, in compliance with the EC Directive, the British policy was adapted to include work of equal value. Currently the three individual policies apply to all types of employment, although the British law initially excluded female-intensive industries from compliance.

One difference that is found among the policies is how general or specific the target of discrimination is. While the British and New Zealand policies prohibit discrimination against both sexes, the Irish law focuses on discrimination against women specifically.

Moving on to the Mediterranean nations, we find equal rights provisions included in their national constitutions. However, all four nations found it necessary to formulate legislation prohibiting discrimination and requiring equal pay. Originally the Spanish policy required equal pay for equal work, while the policies of the other three nations proposed equal pay for work of equal value. Eventually, to comply with the EC Directive, the

Spanish policy adjusted the statement to equal pay for work of equal value.

There are differences among the policies. The Spanish and Italian laws protect all types of employment, while the Portuguese and Greek laws limit the types of jobs to which the laws apply. We also find that, eventually, the Spanish, Greek, and Italian policies focused on discrimination against women, while the Portuguese law took a more general approach and addressed discrimination against all citizens.

Studies comparing the political and societal conditions in the Scandinavian countries conclude that this group of nations shares a number of similar characteristics. However, from this analysis, specific differences among the equal wage policies of the four nations can be noted. Although the four current national laws target discrimination against men and women, the preliminary Swedish law focused on discrimination against women specifically. We also find that the Swedish and Danish policies propose equal pay for the same or like work, while Norway's law requires equal pay for work of equal value, and the law in Iceland suggests equal pay for work of equal value or comparable work. It is also noted that the Swedish and Icelandic policies cover all forms of employment, while the policies of Norway and Denmark exclude certain jobs from compliance. From this examination it appears that the differences among the policies are more noticeable despite the insistence of previous research proclaiming the vast similarities among the Scandinavian nations.

To analyze the final group of European nations, it may be advantageous to divide the four nations into two subgroups, one consisting of Germany and Austria and the other consisting of France and the Netherlands. In both Germany and Austria, equality of wages is not only mentioned in the national constitution, but both nations formulated laws around the same time that target the issue of discrimination against all citizens. The laws of both nations require equal pay for work of equal value. However, the German law applies to all jobs, while the Austrian law does not cover certain types of employment.

Upon examination of France and the Netherlands, we find that the national equal wage policies of these two nations were both formulated in the early to mid-1970s. Both policies target discrimination against women specifically and propose equal pay for work of equal value. One difference between these two policies is that the French law, like the German law, applies to all types of employment, while the Dutch law, like the Austrian law, excludes certain types of employment from coverage.

Although the Japanese law is analyzed separately from the other national policies, it is similar to many of the other policies. Like Germany, Austria, France, and the Mediterranean nations the Japanese constitution includes a provision for equality for all citizens. The national law, one of the earliest formulated wage equality laws requires equal pay for equal or same work, like the laws of the United States, Ireland, New Zealand, Sweden, and Denmark. The law targets discrimination against all citizens, like many of the other laws, and covers all types of employment.

Besides the similarities found within the groups of nations, we also find similarities among most or all of the nations. We notice that the policies have some oversight mechanism (commissions, ministries, or tribunals) and/or enforcement measures (litigation or fines) to encourage compliance. It is also obvious that job segregation has a profound influence on wage inequality in most of the nations. This labor force condition appears to be the main reason that researchers argue for expanding employment opportunities for women to correct wage disparities. An overview of the different policy components for each of the 18 countries is presented in Figure 4.1

Figure 4.1
Equal Wage Policies

	sub-national legislation	purpose of policy	coverage of policy (jobs)	phasing-in period	target	included in constitution
U.S.	yes	EPEW	some	no	both sexes	no
Canada	yes	EPEW to EPEV	some	no	both sexes	no
Britain	no	EPEW to EPEV	all	yes	both sexes	no
Ireland	no	EPEW	all	yes	women	no
New Zealand	no	EPEW	all	yes	both sexes	no
Spain	no	EPEW to EPEV	all	no	women	yes
Portugal	no	EPEV	some	no	both sexes	yes
Greece	no	EPEV	some	no	women	yes
Italy	no	EPEW	all	no	women	yes

Sweden	no	EPEW	all	no	both sexes	no
Iceland	no	EPCW	all	no	both sexes	no
Norway	no	EPEV	some	no	both sexes	no
Denmark	no	EPEW	some	no	both sexes	no
Germany	no	EPEV	all	no	both sexes	yes
Austria	no	EPEV	some	no	both sexes	yes
France	no	EPEV	all	no	women	yes
Nether-lands	no	EPEV	some	no	women	no
Japan	no	EPEW	all	no	both sexes	yes

EPEW = Equal Pay for Equal Work
EPEV = Equal Pay for Equal Value
EPCW = Equal Pay for Comparable Worth

NOTE

1. The 11 categories include those employed in the following manner: in an executive, administrative, or professional capacity; as outside sales personnel; by any retail or service establishment when a majority of the annual dollar income for sales of goods and services is made within the state; by a recreational or amusement establishment; by certain manufacturing retailers; in specific fishing and seafood enterprises; in specific types of agricultural activities; by local newspapers; by small, independently owned public telephone companies; as a seaman on a non-American vessel; or in casual, domestic employment such as baby-sitting or companionship services for those unable to care for themselves (Greenberger, 1980).

Chapter 5

Results of the Analyses

As noted previously, statistical analysis of these data involves two major components. The first analysis (Analysis I) examines the relationship between the number of female policy makers in a country and the presence or absence of a variety of policies comprising two separate categories (i.e., employment and wage protection policy and social policy) of special interest to women. The second analysis (Analysis II) focuses on the relationship between the proportion of female policymakers and the presence and comprehensiveness of one specific policy, equal wage legislation, that is assumed to be highly important to women.

Time-series cross-sectional (TSCS) procedures were used to examine the effects of the independent variables on the dependent variables over time, and across nations. As other researchers note (Friedland & Sanders, 1985; Alvarez et al., 1991; Hicks & Swank, 1992; Pampel, 1993; Hicks, 1994), TSCS data typically violate assumptions underlying ordinary least squares estimation; therefore, the potential for autoregression, heteroscedasticity, and contemporaneously/cross-sectionally correlated errors exists. The Parks generalized least squares approach to time-series analysis deals with the typical problems associated with TSCS data; therefore, the Parks approach is used for this study.[1]

In drawing samples for the two separate analyses (I and II), we begin with 22 industrialized, capitalist democracies and focus on data over a 35-year time period. The number of these countries available for examination in Analysis II (involving equal wage legislation) is reduced to 18 due to the lack of comparability of the policy measures in place in Australia, Belgium, Finland, and Switzerland (see chapter 3). However, as mentioned previously, three of the nations in both pools (Greece, Portugal, and Spain) were not democracies throughout the time period; thus, these countries may be included in either sample only for the years of democratic rule. Because the Parks method requires an equal number of observations for each cross-section, the consequent problem of missing data (years) is addressed in two ways. First, the examination is performed using all of the nations but omitting the years during which Greece, Portugal, and Spain were not democracies; the relevant time period under this approach consequently is limited to the years 1976–1994 for 22 (Analysis I) and 18 (Analysis II) nations. The second approach to the problem uses the full 35-year period but omits the nations (Greece, Portugal, and Spain) that were not democracies during some of this period. The resulting samples under this approach consist of 19 (Analysis I) and 15 nations (Analysis II), respectively, over the full 35-year period.

The first approach allows us to keep the three Mediterranean nations in the study despite the absence of data for these nations during their nondemocratic years. Due to specific national characteristics that are associated with these nations, such as level of Catholicism or socialist influence in government (see chapter 3), it is important to include the three nations in the study to expand the research across different countries that have varying political, religious, and socioeconomic features. Inclusion of these countries allows a better test of the hypothesized relationship between the increase of female policymakers and policy adoption.

Yet it is also important to analyze the relationship between the independent and dependent variables over the appropriate time period. Female representation in policy-making positions begins to appear in the 1960s in countries around the world, as does the enactment of the specific policies that make up the two general policy areas in this research. Therefore, it is important to include the 1960s in this study despite the lack of data for the three Mediterranean nations. Thus, the second approach to the missing data problem, utilizing the 1960–1994 time period without the three Mediterranean nations, is also desirable.

Hence, the potential samples at this juncture for Analysis I consist of (*a*) 22 nations during the period 1976–1994 and (*b*) 19 nations (sample Ia minus Greece, Portugal, and Spain) for the full period 1960–1994; for Analysis II, the potential samples are (*a*) eighteen nations during the period 1976–1994 and (*b*) 15 nations (sample IIa minus Greece, Portugal, and Spain) for the full period 1960–1994. However, comparison of results between Analysis I, sample (*a*) and (*b*), and between Analysis II, sample (*a*) and (*b*) would be confounded in each case by the fact that each subsample varies according to both the number of countries and the period considered; inconsistencies in results could thus be a function of *either* time or country effects. Hence, one final adjustment in the structure of the analysis has been made to enhance interpretation of the results: the longer time frame (1960–1994) in each analysis (I and II) has been divided into two separate time periods (1960–1975 and 1976–1994) for analysis. As a result, in Analysis I, comparisons can be made between the 22-nation sample with the 1976–1994 time period and the 19 nation sample with the 1976–1994 time period. In addition the 19-nation sample during the 1976–1994 time period can be compared with the same nation sample in the earlier time period (1960–1975). Likewise, in Analysis II, comparisons can be made between the 18-nation and 15-nation samples during the 1976–1994 period, as well as between the two separate time periods for the 15-nation sample only.

THE FIRST ANALYSIS

Using the cross-national sample, Analysis I examines the effect of female representation on two general types of policy that are important to women: employment and wage protection policy and social policy. The social policy measure is broken down into two separate measures. The three dependent variables that operationalize the two general types of policy are interval-level measures of the number of specific policies in these two broad areas that are present or absent in each country in each year. For these three measures, a 0 signifies the lack of a policy in a given year, while a 1 indicates the existence of a policy in a given year. The assigned values for the various policies in the two general policy areas are summed for each nation in each year, creating three scales that range from 0 through 4 (the second social policy variable) or 5 (the employment and wage protection policy variable and the first social policy variable).

The employment and wage protection policy variable is composed of laws that advance employment equality and protection. This variable counts the presence or absence of equal wage policy, equal opportunity for women in employment policy, maternity leave policy, parental leave policy and child care policy in each year for each nation. The two social policy variables consist of policies that protect the legal, personal, and educational rights of women. To operationalize the first social policy variable, the presence or absence of divorce/marriage policy, family/child responsibility policy, domestic violence/rape policy, abortion rights policy, and equality in education policy are counted for each nation in each year. Due to the previously explained (see chapter 3) contradictory influence of the Catholic variable on one of the policies included in the social policy variable (abortion rights policy), a second social policy variable excludes that policy from the measurement of the dependent variable.

Frequency Discussion

Table 5.1 presents the means and standard deviations for the employment and wage protection policy variable and both social policy variables during both time periods (1960–1975 and 1976–1994). Earlier, the study suggested that contradictions in the literature are partially due to the use of various policies as dependent variables; thus, the comparability of results may be questioned. When analyzing multiple nations, it must be considered that the type of policy utilized in the research may influence the level of support differently in each nation; thus, some policies may be considered higher priority women's policies (reproductive policies) in certain nations rather than as basic women's interests (child care). In addition, certain countries may be more supportive of one type of policy due to the influence of national characteristics associated with segments of the population (e.g., a high percentage of women in the labor force could influence support for child care or equal wage policies), culture, or religion. To distinguish differences in levels of support that may be due to the type of policy being analyzed, this study categorizes the policies into two broad areas: employment and wage protection policies and social policies.

By examining the data in Table 5.1, we find that the frequency distributions of some of the nations justify the decision to analyze the policies separately. The means for the dependent variables in three of these nations demonstrate that certain nations are at the high end of the employment and wage protection policy average scores but at the middle or at the low end of the social policy average scores (i.e., Australia, Canada, Finland). Conversely, the opposite is found in Britain; the social policy scores for this nation are at the high end, while the employment and wage protection scores are in the midrange. The differences in the average country scores on the policy variables and in the country rankings on the different policy variables support the decision to separate the policy types for analysis.

It is expected that most of the nations will have low mean scores for the policy variables in the 1960–1975 time frame due to the limited female influence on the policy-making process resulting from the lack of, or small percentage of, female policymakers. Likewise, as the percentage of female policymakers increases through the 1970s, 1980s, and 1990s, we would expect the mean scores to be higher for the policy variables in the later (1976–1994) time period. However, the frequencies in Table 5.1 reveal that four of the nations have considerably higher policy

Table 5.1
Means and (Standard Deviations) for Dependent Variables for Analysis I

Country	Employment and Wage Policy		Social Policy I		Social Policy II	
	1960-75	1976-94	1960-75	1976-94	1960-75	1976-94
Australia	.88 (1.63)	4.58 (.51)	0 (0)	2.16 (1.46)	0 (0)	2.16 (1.46)
Austria	.13 (.34)	4 (1)	1.13 (.34)	3.26 (.73)	1 (0)	2.26 (.73)
Belgium	.06 (.25)	3.53 (1.17)	0 (0)	2.58 (2.06)	0 (0)	2.32 (1.77)
Canada	.63 (.96)	3.21 (.54)	.44 (.51)	1.79 (1.03)	0 (0)	.79 (1.03)
Denmark	0 (0)	3.42 (1.22)	1 (1.26)	3.32 (.48)	.88 (1.09)	2.32 (.48)
Finland	1.38 (1.02)	4.32 (.67)	.38 (.50)	2.74 (1.28)	0 (0)	1.74 (1.28)
France	.88 (.81)	4.53 (.77)	.13 (.5)	3.95 (1.27)	.06 (.25)	2.95 (1.27)
Germany	.5 (.52)	3.53 (1.61)	0 (0)	3.74 (.93)	0 (0)	2.74 (.93)
Greece	n.a.	2.79 (2.42)	n.a.	3.32 (1.89)	n.a.	2.84 (1.46)
Iceland	.19 (.40)	4.16 (.76)	1.06 (.25)	3 (0)	1 (0)	2 (0)

Ireland	.13 (.34)	3.84 (1.42)	.19 (.40)	2.31 (1.29)	.19 (.40)	2.32 (1.29)
Italy	.5 (.82)	4.32 (.75)	.88 (.5)	3.16 (.6)	.88 (.5)	2.26 (.45)
Japan	1.25 (.45)	2.89 (1.1)	1.31 (.48)	3.31 (.48)	.31 (.48)	2.32 (.48)
Netherlands	.63 (.62)	3 (.67)	.56 (.51)	3.37 (1.07)	.56 (.51)	2.63 (.68)
New Zealand	.25 (.45)	3 (1.49)	0 (0)	3.26 (1.24)	0 (0)	2.32 (1.16)
Norway	.06 (.25)	4.63 (1.12)	1 (0)	4.42 (1.02)	1 (0)	3.42 (1.02)
Portugal	n.a.	3.79 (1.51)	n.a.	3.68 (1.57)	n.a.	3.11 (1.1)
Spain	n.a.	3.47 (1.90)	n.a.	2.32 (1.67)	n.a.	1.79 (1.23)
Sweden	1.13 (.34)	4.53 (1.02)	.88 (.72)	4.47 (.84)	.88 (.72)	3.47 (.84)
Switzerland	.31 (.48)	2.68 (.58)	1 (0)	2.63 (.9)	0 (0)	1.63 (.9)
United Kingdom	.44 (.63)	2.79 (.92)	1.44 (.146)	4.16 (.37)	.88 (1.02)	3.16 (.37)
United States	1.56 (.81)	3.26 (.81)	.69 (1.08)	3.42 (.61)	.5 (.73)	2.42 (.61)
Full Sample	.54 (.75)	3.64 (1.34)	.66 (.8)	3.26 (1.30)	.47 (.62)	2.42 (1.14)

mean scores than the full sample for the 1960–1975 period. Previous research (Haavio-Mannila et al., 1985; Karvonen & Selle, 1995) suggests that we can expect higher mean scores for two of these nations (Finland and Sweden) because of the early female influence on policy making that resulted from the earlier access of women to Finnish and Swedish representation. However, frequencies for two of the other nations (Japan and the United States) present unexpectedly high policy mean scores in the early time period (for Japan, the scores for employment and wage protection policy and the first social policy are high; for the United States, the score for employment and wage protection policy is higher than that of any other nation). These unexpectedly high scores may be due to two reasons. First, the high scores for both nations could be the result of efforts to *protect* women in employment and society rather than to guarantee economic and social equality. The policies would not expand opportunities for more women; they would protect those women who must work, must support themselves, are abused, and so forth. Second, the existence of these policies in both countries may be symbolic; both nations may have encouraged the passage of these policies to appear more dedicated to the equality of all citizens. Thus, the policies may lack necessary enforcement or oversight provisions that would make them effective.

To compare the three general policy-dependent variables, the correlations for the three variables during both time frames (1960–1975 and 1976–1994) are presented in Figures 5.1 and 5.2. During the 1960–1975 time period, the employment and wage protection policy variable is only modestly correlated with the social policy variables; the policy variable scales are measuring two distinct policy categories. However, since both social policy variables include four of the same policies in the construction of the scales used to measure the variables, the two social policy variables are highly correlated with one another, as we expect them to be.

Figure 5.2 presents the correlations for the same three dependent variables for the 1976–1994 time frame. As we find in

Figure 5.1
Correlation Analysis for Analysis I (1960–1975)

	Employment Policy	Social Policy I	Social Policy II
Employ. Policy	1.00		
Social Policy I	0.29	1.00	
Social Policy II	0.13	0.87	1.00

Figure 5.2
Correlation Analysis for Analysis I (1976–1994)

	Employment Policy	Social Policy I	Social Policy II
Employ. Policy	1.00		
Social Policy I	0.65	1.00	
Social Policy II	0.62	0.94	1.00

the earlier time period, both social policy variables are highly correlated. However, in contrast to the correlations for the earlier time period, the employment and wage protection variable is strongly correlated with both social policy variables during the 1976–1994 period. Rather than measuring two distinct policy categories, these correlations suggest that the employment and wage protection scale and the social policy scales in this later time period are not entirely distinctive policy measures. Instead, in the second time period, individual countries are more likely to score at comparable levels on all three variables. During the second time period, then, the three scales may be providing three ways of measuring one type of policy: women's issue policy.

Three separate multivariate regressions were run for each of the three policy variables considered in Analysis I: one each for the 22-nation sample during the 1976–1994 time period; one each for the 19-nation sample from 1960–1975; and one each for the 19-nation sample from 1976–1994. Tables 5.2–5.4 show the results of the TSCS regressions, utilizing the three dependent variables. The independent variable of most interest in this research—percentage of female policymakers (measured with a four-year lag)—proves to be highly significant in the hypothesized direction, in each time period, and for every sample for each of these three policy indicators.[2]

Thus, all nine of the regressions support the hypothesis that female policy-making representation is associated with policies that are beneficial to women, including policies that target employment and wage protection as well as social issues. Furthermore, because female representation levels are lagged four years behind all other variables, these significant results lend support to our contention that some time in office may be needed to learn the policy-making process and acquire the knowledge and resources to influence it.

Two of the control variables, percentage of female union membership and a binary variable to determine collective bargaining influence, were only included in the regressions utilizing the employment policy variable (Table 5.2). In all three regressions in this case, the variable measuring the percentage of female union membership is statistically significant at the .01 level in the hypothesized direction. These findings support previous research (Cook, 1980; Jonasdóttir, 1988) showing the composition of union membership to have an effect on policies that the unions work for; in this case, higher female membership is associated with more employment and wage policies that are of potential benefit to women.[3] The collective bargaining variable is included in the analysis of employment policy to control for the influence that this different method of policy making might

Table 5.2
Dependent Variable: Employment and Wage Protection Policy
Parameter Estimates and (Standard Errors)

Variable	22 nations 1976-94	19 nations 1960-75	19 nations 1976-94
% Female Policy-makers	.007817 (.001)**	.022717 (.001)**	.009894 (.002)**
Female Heads of Gov't	-.148943 (.020)**	000000 (000)	-.130480 (.030)**
% Catholics	-.002396 (.001)**	.001212 (.000)**	.001949 (.001)
Party I.D.	-.007298 (.006)	-.052235 (.003)**	-.043578 (.010)**
% Socialists	-.001633 (.000)**	-.000324 (.000)**	.001704 (.000)**
% Female Union Membership	.007880 (.001)**	.016529 (.002)**	.023457 (.002)**
% Females in the Labor Force	.034982 (.003)**	.011076 (.001)**	.018165 (.004)**
% Females of Childbearing Age	.131254 (.014)**	.211021 (.005)**	.110456 (.009)**
Collective Bargaining	.449717 (.036)**	.952597 (.011)**	.486164 (.073)**
GDP	-.000092 (.000)**	-.000007 (.000)*	-.000099 (.000)**

** significant at the < .01 level
* significant at the < .05 level

have on policy outcomes in this particular arena. The three regressions that include this control variable indicate that it also is statistically significant in the hypothesized direction, suggesting that this method of policy formulation can result in employment and wage protection policy output that is beneficial to female members of the population.

Upon examination of the other control variables used in studying all three policy variables, we find mixed results depending on the general policy type (employment or social) being analyzed. The female head of government variable is statistically significant in almost all of the regressions at the .01 to .05 levels, except for the analysis of the second social policy variable using the 19-nation sample during the 1976–1994 time period.[4] However, when using the employment and wage protection policy variable, the female head of government variable is significant in the negative direction rather than in the hypothesized positive direction. According to these results, nations with male heads of government were more likely to produce employment policies that benefited women in these countries during the 1976–1994 time period. During those years when nations had female heads of government, fewer employment policies benefiting women were in place. The explanation for these negative results may be that male heads of government place greater importance than do female heads of government on employment issues for both women and men.[5]

On the other hand, the results using the social policy indicators (Table 5.3) show the female head of government variable to be significant in the hypothesized positive direction; when a nation has a female head of government, the social policy outputs tend to be more advantageous to women. This supports our expectation that female prime ministers would be more supportive of women's social policy issues; they may also select cabinet members who share their support for women's social issues.

Mixed results dependent on the policy type are also found using the variable measuring the percentage of women of childbearing years. When analyzed with the employment and wage

Table 5.3
Dependent Variable: Social Policy w/Abortion Policy Parameter Estimates and (Standard Errors)

Variable	22 nations 1976-94	19 nations 1960-75	19 nations 1976-94
% Female Policy-makers	.013341 (.001)**	.013117 (.001)**	.016104 (.000)**
Female Heads of Gov't	.093880 (.034)**	000000 (000)	.085373 (.001)**
% Catholics	.000476 (.001)	.000222 (.000)	.002788 (.000)**
Party I.D.	-.013870 (.006)*	-.055446 (.001)**	.000320 (.000)
% Socialists	.000143 (.000)	.000427 (.000)**	-.000194 (.000)**
% Females in the Labor Force	.081347 (.003)**	.020139 (.001)**	.073591 (.000)**
% Females of Childbearing Age	-.014658 (.015)**	.127886 (.017)**	-.016882 (.000)**
GDP	-.000059 (.000)**	-.000004 (.000)**	-.000062 (.000)**

** significant at the <.01 level
* significant at the <.05 level

protection policy variable, using both samples and both time periods, this control variable is statistically significant at the .01 level and in the hypothesized positive direction, suggesting that nations provide more policies that address employment protection and advancement opportunities when there are more women of childbearing age. We also find that this variable is statistically significant at the .01 level in the hypothesized direction in the analysis of the first social policy variable using the nineteen nation sample and 1960–1975 time period. According to these results, during the 1960–1975 time period, nations provided more social policies (including abortion rights) that benefited women when there were more women in this age group.

However, when analyzed with the first social policy variable during the 1976–1994 time period and with the second social policy variable across both samples and time periods, the percentage of women of childbearing years, though still statistically significant at the .01 and .05 levels in the five sets of regressions, is negatively related to the two sets of social policies. Thus, the lower the percentage of women in this age group at any given time, the more women's social policies in place. In four of the regressions using the 1976–1994 time frame, this apparent anomaly might be a function of the examined time period rather than the influence of female constituents in their childbearing years. The presence of social policies in these later years might have resulted from the need for national policymakers to protect women's rights in light of the attention given to the emerging women's movements. Unfortunately we are at a loss to explain the negative results for the 19-nation/1960–1975 regression with the second social policy variable.

These findings provide overall support for some previous research. For example, the variable measuring the percentage of women in the labor force is statistically significant in a positive direction at the .01 and .05 levels, with the three measures of the dependent variables using both time periods in eight of the nine regressions. These results support the earlier claims of such analysts as Anderson (1975), Welch (1977), Gurin (1987), and Githens (1994) that public policies reflect changing societal conditions, such as the growing female labor force activity. The strong convergence between the preponderance of evidence here and earlier research in this case leaves less concern over the one negative result between female labor force participation and so-

Table 5.4
Dependent Variable: Social Policy Excluding Abortion Policy
Parameter Estimates and (Standard Errors)

Variable	22 nations 1976-94	19 nations 1960-75	19 nations 1976-94
% Female Policy-makers	.012483 (.001)**	.009277 (.000)**	.015907 (.000)**
Female Heads of Gov't	.128271 (.027)**	000000 (000)	.024218 (.017)
% Catholics	.002594 (.000)**	-.002803 (.000)**	.003932 (.000)**
Party I.D.	-.002594 (.004)	-.012876 (.001)**	.003323 (.003)
% Socialists	-.000350 (.000)*	-.000191 (.000)**	-.000128 (.000)
% Females in the Labor Force	.063554 (.002)**	-.001365 (.000)**	.050478 (.001)**
% Females of Childbearing Age	-.054388 (.005)**	-.024173 (.008)**	-.058967 (.005)**
GDP	-.000075 (.000)**	-.000025 (.000)**	-.000081 (.000)**

** significant at the <.01 level
* significant at the <.05 level

cial policy, excluding abortion policy, during the earliest time period (Table 5.4). We might speculate that strong female labor force participation during the earliest time period drew legislative attention first to enactment of policies supportive of continued labor force participation by women, such as employment and wage policies and abortion rights policies, delaying or impeding enactment of more traditional social rights policies.

Yet some of these findings contradict other research. As mentioned earlier, many analysts expect the dominant political party to have a major influence on policy formation, with many scholars (Hibbs, 1977; Norris, 1987) contending that liberal parties will be more supportive of liberal policies; generally, women's issue policies are categorized as liberal policies (Leader, 1977; Norris, 1987). However, the results of five of the regressions[6] suggest the opposite. The analyses of the employment policy variable without the Greece, Portugal, and Spain data, the first social policy variable including the data from the 22-nation/1976–1994 sample, and the 19-nation/1960–1975 analyses of both social policy measures produce results that are statistically significant at the .01 and .05 levels in the negative direction. According to these results, conservative parties in power are more strongly associated with both employment and social policies that benefit women.

The reason for the negative results may be attributed to the different policy variables and the methods used to measure the variables. For example, Hibbs (1977) analyzes the effects of political parties on liberal macroeconomic policies (unemployment and inflation policies) and uses interval-level data measuring the percentages of unemployment and inflation. In a more similar study to this one, Norris (1987) utilizes four individual policies that are included in the policy type variables of this study: abortion rights, child care, education opportunities for women, and maternity services. However, she analyzes the policies as individual policy variables, using interval-level data to measure the abortion rate, child care facilities, rate of college education for women, and maternity services rather than combining the individual policies into two interval scales to measure the presence or absence of the policies in the general policy categories. Although liberal parties may be more supportive of the individual interval-level policy measurements used in the Hibbs and Norris studies, the scales used here to measure various individual policies within two general policy categories may cause the seemingly contradictory results.

In addition, the nation sample and time frame of the analysis may also affect the results. Hibbs' includes 12 European and North American nations over a 28-year time period, 1948–1975 (rather than the 22-nation/1960–1994 time period used in this study). While Norris uses the same 22 nations found in this study, her sample also includes Luxembourg and Israel and her time frame ranges from 1970 to the mid-1980s.

The results also contradict the major body of research (Dye, 1966; Dye, 1976; Wilensky, 1975; King, 1981) suggesting that the economic growth of a nation has a positive effect on employment and social policies that are especially important to women. According to the nine regressions that reveal the measure of gross domestic product per capita to be statistically significant at the .01 to .05 levels, the relationship is an inverse one, signifying that countries with lower levels of economic growth are more likely to formulate the types of policies studied here.

The explanation for these seemingly contrary results may once again be due to differences in the analyzed policies and operationalization of the policy variables. The Dye (1966) study included over 90 policy output measures dealing with health, education, and welfare issues (among others); Wilensky (1975) utilized education and housing policy expenditures for his dependent variables. Neither study analyzed the effect of economic growth on the women's issue policies included here. Further, even research addressing the link between the Gross National Product (GNP) and policy expenditures has not demonstrated uniformly consistent findings. Castles (1982), for example, found GNP to be inversely related to spending on education, income maintenance, and health in the OECD nations over the time period from the early 1960s to the 1970s. Perhaps his hypothesis that political determinants that influence changes in resource commitments differ depending on the types of programs is the more appropriate one, with these results lending additional support to his argument.

Two other control variables show mixed relationships with the dependent variables. Theoretically, Catholic nations are expected to be more traditional in their response to female employment, child care, divorce, and reproductive freedom (Blau & Ferber, 1992; Norris, 1987; Sapiro, 1981). Therefore, the percentage of Catholics in a nation is expected to have a negative relationship with policies that target women's personal and professional rights. Two of the regressions demonstrate this hypothesized relationship. The analysis of the employment policy variable using the data from all 22 nations and the analysis of the second social policy variable with the 19-nation sample during the 1960–1975 time period show the percentage of Catholics to be statistically significant at the .01 level. These results support earlier studies that contend that nations with less Catholic influence prioritize policies that enhance and protect the rights of women more than nations with greater Catholic influenced do. However, the analyses of the employment and wage protection variable with the 19-nation/1960–1975 data, the first social policy variable with the 19-nation/1976–1994 data, and the second social policy variable using the 22-nation and 19-nation samples during 1976–1994 suggest a positive relationship. In this case the percentage of Catholics variable is statistically significant at the .01 level; the stronger the Catholic influence, the more likely the nation will have policies that protect the legal, personal, and educational rights of women, excluding reproductive rights.[7]

The results for the analysis of the employment and wage protection variable with the 19-nation/1960–1975 data might possibly be explained by the conservative attitude of the Catholic Church during that time period. The policies used to operationalize the employment and wage protection variable could have been viewed as "protective measures" for women in the labor force during this early period rather than as methods of promoting equality between the sexes. If the Catholic Church's intention was to protect the rights of motherhood for those women who had to work, it is possible that the church would support such policies and would encourage its followers to do the same. In this light the relationship between Catholicism and employment and wage protection policy compliments the previously disclosed, unexpectedly high scores of Japan and the United States on this policy variable during the earlier time period. This suggests that the employment and wage policy indicators measured here might very well represent very different things to different groups or countries or to the same group or country at different points in time.

Similarly, for the analyses using both social policy variables, the results could explain the protective attitude of the Catholic Church toward single, divorced, or abused women. Those women viewed as abused or abandoned by their husbands would need legal protection for themselves and their children. They would also need further education to support themselves and their children. Once again the support of the Catholic Church would be due to its intention to protect women and children.

Finally, the analysis provides mixed findings in regard to the effects of the percentage of socialists in the government. Previous research suggests that nations with influential socialist parties provide more opportunities for women and are more likely to support policies that benefit women (Norris, 1987; Skjeie, 1993). As a consequence it was expected that the relationship between the percentage of socialists in the government and the dependent variables would be a positive one. The analyses of the employment policy variable using data from the 19-nation/1976–1994 sample, and the first social policy variable with data from the 19-nation/1960–1975 sample, support this expectation. However, the analyses of the employment and wage protection policy variable with the 22-nation/1976–1994 and the 19-nation/1960–1994 samples, the first social policy variable using the 19-nation/1976–1994 sample, and the analyses of the second social policy variable with the data from the 22-nation/1976–1994 and 19-nation/1960–1975 samples suggest the opposite relationship. In these five regressions, lower percentages of socialists in the government are associated with more policies that are beneficial to women.

Though unexpected, these negative results are similar to results found by Keman (1982) and Eduards et al. (1985). In the Keman study, the percentage of socialist seats in parliament had a negative effect on the change in spending on education, income maintenance, and health policy; however, the negative results were not statistically significant. The lack of significant results supports the earlier mentioned (see chapter two) work of Parkin (1971) and Jackman (1980); both researchers propose that the effect of socialist party strength on economic equality policies is almost nonexistent. The Eduards research provides a specific example of a negative relationship between socialist party dominance in government and women's issue policy. According to the authors, the Swedish Act of 1980 (a bill providing active measures promoting equality between the sexes) faced strong opposition from the socialist government due to union and employer influence on the socialist party. The act was finally implemented when a nonsocialist government supported its enforcement.

As mentioned earlier the explanation for the divergent results may be due to the policy measures, time frames or nation samples of the studies. The Norris (1987) study used a different method of measuring policy outcome as well as a different time period for the analysis. The Skjeie (1993) study also used a different time period in addition to focusing on only one nation, which was Norway. All three of these factors may have contributed to the unexpected negative results.

Again, when comparing the regression results, we find that some of the inconsistencies in relationship direction and statistical significance can be attributed to the countries included in the sample or the time frame of the sample. The analyses of the employment and wage protection policy variable suggest that the inclusion of Greece, Portugal, and Spain influences the relationship between the percentage of Catholics variable and this dependent variable. Inclusion of the three Catholic nations results in the expected negative relationship between the variables, supporting research (Norris, 1987; Blau & Ferber, 1992) that demonstrates the Catholic nations' conservative attitude about the expansion of women's rights. In addition, the inclusion of these three nations and the use of the earlier time period (1960–1975) results in an unexpected negative relationship between the percentage of socialists in the government variable and the employment and wage dependent variable. Although scholars (Norris, 1987; Skjeie, 1993) have presented evidence of socialist parties' support for women's issues, these studies examined European nations other than Greece, Portugal, or Spain (Skjeie, 1993) or took place during later time periods, specifically the 1980s for Norris and the 1990s for Skjeie. Therefore, the negative results may be attributed to the differences in country sample or time frame.

In analyzing the first social policy dependent variable, different time periods affect the percentage of females of childbearing age variable; during the earlier period, a positive relationship is found between this independent variable and the dependent variable, while during the 1976–1994 period a negative relationship is found. Both country effects and time effects are found in the estimates for the party identification variable and the percentage of socialists variable.

Similar inconsistencies are found in the analyses of the second social policy dependent variable. The time frame used in the analyses affects the percentage of Catholics variable as well as the percentage of females in the labor force variable. For the party identification variable, inconsistencies in relationship direction can be attributed to both time effects and country effects.

When we compare the results of the main policy types, the relationships between certain control variables and the dependent variables are consistent. The party dominance variable and gross domestic product per capita variable are negatively linked with both the employment and wage protection variable and both social policy variables. Based on this information, employment and wage protection policies and social policies are more likely to exist in less prosperous nations with conservative parties in power. Similarly, the relationships between the percentage of women in the labor force and both policy types are consistently positive when abortion policy is excluded from the social policy scale (social policy II). This suggests that nations with higher percentages of females in the labor force are likely to have more employment and social policies that benefit women; however, when abortion policies are included in the measurement of the social policy, the time period influences the analysis, resulting in a negative relationship.

For one of the control variables, female heads of government, the results suggest inconsistencies in the direction of the relationship, depending on the policy type. According to the data, the female heads of government variable is negatively related to the employment and wage protection policy variable but positively related to the social policy variable. These results indicate that nations with female heads of government were more likely to have social policies and less likely to have employment and wage protection policies.

The results for the other control variables demonstrate the time period and country sample effects mentioned earlier. Analyzing data from the earlier time period, or including or excluding certain nations from the samples, produces mixed results regardless of the policy type. Both positive and negative relationships are found between the two policy types and the control variables measuring the percentage of Catholics, percentage of socialists in the government, and percentage of women of childbearing age.

THE SECOND ANALYSIS

As noted, Analysis I utilizes three dependent variables that measure the presence or absence of multiple policies in two general policy areas of interest to women; one of the variables is employment and wage protection policy. This variable includes specific policies that address employment and wage protection, including equal wage policy.

To examine the effect of female policymakers on the substance of a specific policy rather than on the presence or absence of a variety of policies, Analysis II focuses on one selected policy, equal wage legislation. Since four of the originally analyzed nations formulated their equal wage policies through the collective bargaining process, these four nations are excluded from this analysis; therefore, this part of the study uses a cross-national sample of 18 nations.

For this part of the study, two scales were constructed to estimate the comprehensiveness of the national-level equal wage laws to measure the dependent variable; both scales range from 0 through 3. The first scale measures the progression in the advancement of each specific policy's goals, with 0 signifying no law, 1 signifying a law of equal pay for equal work, 2 signifying a law of equal pay for work of equal value, and 3 signifying a law of equal pay for comparable work. The second scale measures the application of the laws. For this scale, 0 signifies no law, 1 signifies a law focusing on equality for all applying to certain jobs, 2 signifies a law focusing on equality for all applying to all jobs or a law focusing on equal wages for women applying to certain jobs, and 3 signifies a law focusing on equal wages for women applying to all jobs.

In comparison to the employment and wage protection scale used in Analysis I, the two equal wage policy scales are intended to measure the substantive elements of a single policy rather than the existence or lack of various policies. For Analysis I with the employment and wage protection scale, we were searching for evidence of a link between female representation levels and the presence or absence of various policies. The purpose of Analysis II using both equal wage scales is to examine whether female representation levels are linked to differences in the substance of a single policy.

Our first equal wage policy scale assesses the comprehensiveness of the policy according to the stated goals of the legislation. If the stated goal of the policy is to achieve equal pay for equal work, then the policy is determined to be less comprehensive than a policy that is implemented to achieve equal pay for comparable work. As the goals of the policies allow more jobs to be compared to determine the equalization of wages, it is expected that the policies will be considered more comprehensive in the battle against wage inequality.

The second equal wage policy scale assesses the comprehensiveness of the policy according to the scope of application of the policy. For example, policies with general (stressing equality for everyone) applicability would be considered less comprehensive in relation to women's wage equality than those with specific (stressing equal wages for women) applicability. Similarly, policies that apply to all types of employment would be considered more comprehensive than those applying to only certain types of employment. According to this scale, it is expected that as the policies address a more specific approach and apply to all types of employment, the more comprehensive the policy coverage will be.

Frequency Discussion

The means and standard deviations for the two equal wage policy scales during both time periods (1960–1975 and 1976–1994) are presented in Table 5.5. As mentioned in Analysis I, we expect most of the nations to have low mean scores for the policy variables in the 1960–1975 time period due to the limited female influence on policy making during that time span. It is also expected that as the percentage of female policy makers increases through the later time period (1976–1994), the mean scores for the policy variables will be greater. According to the frequencies, only one nation, Japan, has a relatively high mean score for both equal wage policy scales in the early time period. In Analysis I the mean score for the employment and wage protection policy variable was also unexpectedly high for Japan (the other three nations that had higher mean scores in the earlier time period for the employment and wage protection policy variable are either in the expected range or excluded from the sample). The explanation for the high scores in Analysis II, as in

Analysis I, may be due to the belief in Japanese government and society that women in the labor force must be protected. However, with Japan's reputation as a traditional society and the knowledge that Japanese women earn approximately 53% of what their male counterparts earn (Yoko et al., 1994), policies that guarantee equal rights for women in the workplace may be little more than symbolic.

In the later time period we find several unexpected high and low mean scores. Three nations (France, Ireland, and Japan) have unexpected high mean scores for the second equal wage policy scale. All three of these nations are considered traditional societies where women hold few government positions. When these scores are compared to the mean scores for the employment and wage protection policy variable, France is the only one of the three nations with a high mean score for that variable. Despite the French case, the fact that Ireland and Japan have average mean scores for the employment variable indicates that the anomaly may be due to the construction and justification of the second equal wage policy scale, or that the second equal wage policy scale and the employment and wage protection variable scale are providing different policy measures.

When examining the later time period for both equal wage policy scales, five nations show relatively low mean scores. According to Table 5.5, Sweden has an unexpected low score for the first equal wage policy scale. Since Sweden is considered more committed to equal rights and opportunities for women and has a relatively small wage differential, with women earning 85 percent of what men earn (OECD, 1988), than many of the other nations in this study, these low scores seem inaccurate. For the second equal wage policy scale, four nations (Austria, Portugal, Denmark, and Norway) show relatively low scores in the later time period. Due to the strong Catholic influence and traditional character of Austria and Portugal, the low mean scores are not unexpected. However, the low scores of Denmark and Norway seem inaccurate for the same reason given for Sweden. Like Sweden, the governments of Denmark and Norway are commit-

Table 5.5
Means and (Standard Deviations) for Dependent Variables for Analysis II

Country	Equal Wage Policy Scale 1		Equal Wage Policy Scale 2	
	1960-1975	1976-1994	1960-1975	1976-1994
Austria	0 (0)	1.68 (.75)	0 (0)	.84 (.37)
Canada	.31 (.48)	1.95 (.23)	.31 (.48)	1 (0)
Denmark	0 (0)	1 (0)	0 (0)	1 (0)
France	.5 (.89)	2 (0)	.75 (1.34)	3 (0)
Germany	0 (0)	1.58 (.84)	0 (0)	1.58 (.84)
Greece	n.a.	1.16 (1.01)	n.a.	1.16 (1.01)
Iceland	0 (0)	3 (0)	0 (0)	2 (0)
Italy	0 (0)	1.89 (.46)	0 (0)	2.84 (.69)

Japan	1 (0)	1 (0)	2.25 (.45)	3 (0)
Netherlands	.13 (.5)	2 (0)	.13 (.5)	2 (0)
New Zealand	.25 (.45)	1 (0)	.5 (.89)	2 (0)
Norway	0 (0)	1.79 (.63)	0 (0)	.89 (.32)
Portugal	n.a.	1.68 (.75)	n.a.	.84 (.37)
Spain	n.a.	1.16 (.76)	n.a.	1.95 (1.13)
Sweden	0 (0)	.79 (.42)	0 (0)	2.21 (1.23)
United Kingdom	.38 (.5)	1.63 (.5)	.38 (.5)	1.63 (.5)
United States	.81 (.4)	1 (0)	.81 (.4)	1 (0)
Full Sample	.23 (.47)	1.52 (.73)	.36 (.78)	1.77 (.95)

Figure 5.3
Correlation Analysis for Analysis II (1960–1975)

	Employment Policy	Equal Wage I	Equal Wage II
Employ. Policy	1.00		
Equal Wage I	0.71	1.00	
Equal Wage II	0.62	0.92	1.00

ted to equality between the sexes in government, society, and the labor force; as a result laws and practices, such as quotas, in these nations have targeted representation and employment equality.

When we compare the scores for the equal wage scales with the scores for the employment and wage protection policy, all five of the nations with low scores for the equal wage scales have average to high mean scores for the employment and wage protection policy in the 1976–1994 time period (Denmark's is the lowest of the five at 3.42). The differences in mean scores between the employment policy and equal wage policy scales may be due to faulty equal wage scales or the noncomparability of the different types of policy measures.

Another way to determine the differences in policy measures is to examine the correlations of the equal wage scales and the employment and wage protection variable. Because the equal wage policy is one of the five policies included in the general employment and wage protection policy variable, it is expected that the two equal wage scales will correlate with the employment policy variable. When examining the correlations for the early time period in Figure 5.3 (1960–1975) both equal wage scales are correlated with the employment and wage protection variable (the first equal wage scale is more highly correlated with the employment policy variable than the second equal

Figure 5.4
Correlation Analysis for Analysis II (1976–1994)

	Employment Policy	Equal Wage I	Equal Wage II
Employ. Policy	1.00		
Equal Wage I	0.53	1.00	
Equal Wage II	0.41	0.32	1.00

wage scale), supporting our expectation. However, during the later time period reported in Figure 5.4 (1976–1994), the equal wage scales are not as correlated with the employment policy variable, suggesting that the equal wage scales are not as closely related to the general employment and wage protection policy scale during this later time period.

Furthermore, when comparing the correlations between the two equal wage scales, we find that the scales are highly correlated during the 1960–1975 time period; this suggests that the scales are measuring the same or similar policy characteristics that define policy comprehensiveness. However, during the 1976–1994 time period, the equal wage scales are no longer correlated, suggesting that the scales are measuring different characteristics of policy comprehensiveness.

Time-series cross-sectional regression analyses were conducted on the equal wage laws of 18 industrialized democracies to examine the relationship between the independent variables, explained earlier, and the equal wage policy dependent variable. For this part of the study, two scales constructed to estimate the range of application for the national-level equal wage laws measure the dependent variable. The results from the six regressions are presented here. Three of the regressions use the first equal wage scale with the 19-year time period (one including the data for Greece, Portugal, and Spain and one excluding those countries), and the 16-year time period (excluding data from Greece, Portugal, and Spain). The other three regressions were run using the second equal wage scale with the same separate time periods.

Table 5.6 shows the results for the regressions using the first equal wage policy scale with the 18-nation sample during the 1976–1994 time period, the 15-nation sample during the 1960–1975 time period, and the 15-nation sample during the 1976–1994 period. In all three regressions the main independent variable—percentage of female policymakers with a four-year lag—reached an acceptable level of statistical significance at the .01 level; however, the relationship was not in the hypothesized direction. According to these results, nations with higher percentages of female policymakers are less likely to produce equal wage policies that are more progressive, indicated here by the expansion of job categories for wage comparison purposes. Based on these results, it appears that the equal wage policy goals are more limited (comparing same or equal jobs rather than jobs of equal value or comparable value) in nations that have a higher percentage of women in positions who can influence policy formulation and revision. Therefore, these examinations do not support the hypothesis that greater female representation results in more progressive policies addressing wage inequality.

The results for the regressions utilizing the second equal wage policy scale and the same nation sample and time periods are found in Table 5.7. As noted in the analyses of the first equal wage policy scale, the independent variable of most interest is also statistically significant at the .01 level but in the negative direction.[8] Once again it appears that nations with more female policymakers are less likely to have policies that benefit women, such as policy goals that specifically target wage disparities between women and men in all types of employment. Thus, the results for the second analysis also do not support the hypothesis.

The explanation for these negative results may involve the justification of policy characteristics in the construction of the equal wage scales. Although the author explains the policy goals and attributes that are used to designate values for the different

Table 5.6
Dependent Variable: Equal Wage Policy—Scale 1 Parameter
Estimates and (Standard Errors)

Variable	18 nations 1976-94	15 nations 1960-75	15 nations 1976-94
% Female Policy-makers	-.005115 (.000)**	-.007587 (.000)**	-.010776 (.001)**
Female Heads of Gov't	.038177 (.016)*	000000 (000)	-.035163 (.018)
% Catholics	-.001779 (.000)**	.002701 (.000)**	.005502 (.001)**
Party I.D.	.029877 (.002)**	.061040 (.001)**	-.015222 (.003)**
% Socialists	-.001368 (.000)**	-.000541 (.000)**	-.000691 (.000)**
% Female Union Membership	-.001552 (.000)**	-.003122 (.000)**	-.002100 (.001)**
% Females in the Labor Force	.006693 (.001)**	.014049 (.001)**	-.012851 (.002)**
% Females of Childbearing Age	.068051 (.004)**	-.002972 (.005)	.055945 (.003)**
GDP	-.000007 (.000)**	-.000023 (.000)**	.000011 (.000)**

** significant at the < .01 level
* significant at the < .05 level

Table 5.7
Dependent Variable: Equal Wage Policy—Scale 2 Parameter
Estimates and (Standard Errors)

Variable	18 nations 1976-94	15 nations 1960-75	15 nations 1976-94
% Female Policy-makers	-.005563 (.001)**	-.015890 (.000)**	-.006134 (.001)**
Female Heads of Gov't	-.112501 (.019)**	000000 (000)	-.042570 (.035)
% Catholics	-.003084 (.001)**	.005437 (.000)**	.014516 (.001)**
Party I.D.	.032322 (.005)**	.032337 (.001)**	-.009080 (.003)**
% Socialists	.000102 (.000)	.000010 (.000)	.000115 (.000)**
% Female Union - Membership	.007205 (.001)**	-.003699 (.000)**	.003880 (.001)**
% Females in the Labor Force	-.006839 (.002)**	.006480 (.000)**	.011295 (.002)**
% Females of Childbearing Age	.096134 (.006)**	-.083865 (.004)**	.070460 (.006)**
GDP	-.000014 (.000)**	-.000040 (.000)**	-.0000058 (.000)

** significant at the < .01 level
* significant at the < .05 level

policies over the time series, the actual policymakers may not
have considered the differences in terminology in the same
manner. For example, in the first equal wage scale, work of comparable value, which is given a high value of 3, may be considered by policymakers to mean the same as work of equal value,
which is given a value of 2. In the second equal wage policy
scale, equal wage policies that target inequality for both sexes
may mean the same to policymakers as policies that focus on
inequality for women, which is given a greater value than policies targeting inequality for both men and women. Therefore,
the negative results for both equal wage scales may be due to
the construction of the scales.

Another explanation for the negative results may be the lack
of a critical level of representation and the limited seniority that
female policymakers have to influence the wording of the equal
wage policies. The women in policy-making positions may be
more interested in the implementation of various policies that
benefit women rather than in the details of each policy. As these
women gain seniority and more women achieve these positions,
the female influence on policy details may be more apparent.

Many of the other control variables are statistically significant
at the .01 and .05 levels; some of these findings provide support
for previous research. The regression using the first equal wage
scale during the 1976–1994 period using the 18–nation sample
supports research regarding the effects of Catholic influence,
party dominance, percentage of women in the labor force, and
percentage of women of childbearing years; the findings also
support the author's suspicion that a female head of government
will positively influence policy formulation. Based on these results, nations with liberal parties dominating government, less
influence from the Catholic Church, more women in the labor
force, and more women of childbearing age will have more comprehensive equal wage policies. However, the results suggest that
the percentage of socialists in the government, the percentage of
female union membership, and the gross domestic product per
capita are all statistically significant but not in the hypothesized

direction; instead it appears that more socialists in government, higher percentages of female union membership, and greater wealth in a country at any given time are associated with equal wage policy that is less beneficial to women.

The analysis using the same dependent variable and the 15–nation data during the 1960–1975 time period provides less support for the hypothesized effects of control variables. In this case only party dominance and the percentage of women in the labor force are found to be statistically significant at the .01 level in the hypothesized positive direction, indicating that nations with liberal parties in power and stronger female representation in the labor force will have more comprehensive equal wage policies. The percentage of Catholics, percentage of socialists, female union membership, and gross domestic product per capita variables are all statistically significant but not in the hypothesized direction.

When analyzing the same dependent variable with the same nation sample but a different time frame (1976–1994), the females of childbearing age and gross domestic product per capita variables are the only two variables that are statistically significant at the .01 level in the hypothesized positive direction; this suggests that nations with stronger economies and more women in their childbearing years will have more comprehensive equal wage policies. However, once again the percentage of Catholics, percentage of socialists, and female union membership are all statistically significant variables but not in the hypothesized direction. In addition, party dominance and percentage of women in the labor force are also statistically significant in the negative direction, which was not hypothesized.

One reason that certain variables are related to the first equal wage scale but not in the hypothesized direction is due to the difference in dependent policy variables (explained in Analysis I) that have been used in the previous research. The equal wage scales used in this study are not based on the policy variables utilized by other scholars (Dye, 1966; Wilensky, 1975; Keman, 1982; Norris, 1987) as mentioned in chapter three. Furthermore, the analysis of different nation samples (Dye, 1966) and time frames (Keman, 1982; Norris, 1987) could also cause the contradictory results.

Analyzing the relationships between the control variables with the second equal wage scale supplies further evidence for many of the control variables. With the 18 nation/1976–1994 data, the variables operationalizing Catholic influence, political party dominance, percentage of female union membership, and percentage of women of childbearing years are all statistically significant at the .01 level in the expected direction; these results once again indicate that nations with less Catholic influence, stronger liberal parties in government, greater female union membership, and more women of childbearing age will have equal wage policies that are more comprehensive based on the second equal wage scale used here. However, the female head of government indicator, percentage of women in the labor force, and gross domestic product per capita variables are statistically significant in the unexpected negative direction. Based on these findings, nations with female heads of government are less likely to influence the drafting of equal wage policy that directly addresses the wage disparity between women and men for all jobs. It also appears that a high proportion of female laborers and greater national wealth adversely affects equal wage policy.

The 15-nation sample with the 1960–1975 time period provides support for the research on the influence of party dominance and female labor force activity; both variables are statistically significant at the .01 level in the hypothesized positive direction, indicating that liberal parties and female labor membership influence the comprehensiveness of equal wage policies. Other variables, including the percentage of Catholics, female union membership, women of childbearing age, and gross domestic product per capita are statistically significant but not in the expected direction.

Finally, the 15-nation/1976–1994 statistics support the expected results of four of the control variables. Using the second equal wage scale, the percentage of socialists, female union membership, the percentage of women in the labor force, and percentage of women of childbearing years are all statistically significant at the .01 level in the expected positive direction. Once again the influence of socialists in government, women of childbearing age, and female union and labor force strength on policy comprehensiveness is indicated. However, as found in the other analyses, certain variables are statistically significant in the opposite direction: the percentage of Catholics in the positive direction and party dominance in the negative direction.

Unexpected results are found throughout Analysis II. In this analysis, as well as in Analysis I, we note that the use of different policy indicators and measures may be one reason for the contradictory results. The use of changes in welfare and education policy expenditures (Keman, 1982), unemployment and inflation policies (Hibbs, 1977), or specific policy output (Norris, 1987) are different policy measures from the measures used in this study.

In addition, inconsistencies in the direction of the variable relationships may be due to the different country samples and time frames of the analyses. The regressions using the first equal wage policy indicate that the choice of countries included in each sample influences the percentage of Catholics variable. Country and time effects can be found in the party dominance, percentage of women in the labor force, and gross domestic product per capita variables; the results from these three variables indicate that the inclusion of Greece, Portugal, and Spain in the sample or the use of the earlier time period (1960–1975) influences the direction of the variable relationship.

The results using the second equal wage policy dependent variable suggest similar country and time effects. Again the results for the percentage of Catholics variable and the women in the labor force variable indicate that the nation sample used in the analysis affects the outcome. The time frame of the analysis has an effect on the percentage of women of childbearing age variable. Moreover, the results indicate that both country and time period effects influence party dominance and female union membership variables.

As the results for the first equal wage policy scale are examined, we find that the negative relationship between this dependent variable and the primary independent variable, percentage of female policymakers, is consistent throughout the time series. We also find that the links between this policy variable and the percentage of socialists in the government and the percentage of female union membership are also consistently negative through both time periods using both country samples. This suggests that when we use this scale and analyze the influence of the number of female policymakers, socialist government strength, and female union membership on equal wage policy, policy comprehensiveness will be greater when there are fewer female policymakers, a smaller percentage of socialists in the government, and fewer women in the unions.[9]

In the analysis of the second equal wage policy scale, the primary independent variable, percentage of female policymakers, has a negative relationship with this dependent variable throughout the time series. In addition, the female heads of government and the gross domestic product per capita variables are also negatively linked with this policy variable. However, the variable measuring socialist strength in government has a consistently positive relationship with the dependent variable.[10] According to these findings, when the second equal wage policy scale is used to measure policy comprehensiveness, nations with male heads of government, poorer economic conditions, and stronger socialist influence in government are likely to have more comprehensive equal wage policies.

When we compare the results for the two equal wage scales, the only variable that is consistent throughout the time periods for both scales is the percentage of female policymakers. This suggests that, despite the differences in the two equal wage policies, the number of female policymakers has a negative influence on both scales measuring policy comprehensiveness; hence, the more women in policy-making positions, the less comprehensive the equal wage policies will be. As mentioned earlier this may be due to the lack of influence (percentage of representation and seniority) on the writing of equal wage policies that female policymakers have. When comparing the findings for the two equal wage scales with the employment and wage protection variable, none of the variable relationships are consistent across the three policy measures. This is especially important when we examine the primary independent variable: percentage of female policymakers. According to the findings, the number of women in policy-making positions is positively related to the employment and wage protection variable but negatively related to both equal wage policy scales. These results support the contention that the employment variable is measuring something different than the equal wage scales are measuring even though both types of policy measures focus on employment issues.

DISCUSSION

According to these results, the percentage of female policymakers has an effect on the implementation of policies that emphasize women's issues in both employment and social matters. The more female representatives in a nation, the greater the likelihood that the nation will implement policies that are considered more important to women; this includes policies that protect and enhance employment, family responsibility, personal safety, reproductive freedom, and education rights. If this relationship continues, we can expect that more women's issue policies will be implemented as more women achieve policy-making positions.

However, the same cannot be said when analyzing the content of one specific set of policies. Rather, findings for the second analysis indicate that the percentage of female policymakers is negatively related to the substance of a specific policy that is important to women: equal wage policy. Contrary to the given hypothesis, the lesser the representation of female policymakers, the greater the progressiveness or comprehensiveness of national equal wage policies.

According to these findings, female policymakers are more strongly associated with the presence of large numbers of public policies benefiting women than they are with more comprehensive policies, at least in regard to equal wage law; this indicates that female policymakers have an effect on general policy outputs but not on the substance of the policies. The explanation for the statistical outcome may be due to the relatively recent entry and limited proportion of women in the policy-making process. It can be argued that policy comprehensiveness usually increases over time. Considering female policymakers' limited time in office and the small proportion of women in these positions, it is likely that the first step for female officeholders is to get their prioritized policies adopted. After the policies are adopted, then the female policymakers can work at gradually expanding the policy coverage. Therefore, female policymakers would need to hold office for a longer period of time before we would expect to see impacts on the policy comprehensiveness.

Alternatively, the problem may not be due to the presence or absence of female policymakers at all. The problem may be the scales themselves. The policy distinctions employed in constructing the equal wage policy scales may not hold the same significance for those formulating and implementing the policies; therefore, the values associated with these distinctions may not be an accurate measure of the comprehensiveness of the policy. For example, the use of the terms "similar work," "work of equal value," and "work of comparable worth" may be equivalent to those actually writing the policies; thus, the goals or intended comprehensiveness of the policies may be the same despite the use of different terminology. Yet the scoring may differ substantially under this study's operationalization of policy comprehensiveness. The possibility of such weakness in the operationalization of these scales gains support not just from the contradictory findings regarding the effect of our key independent variable on the policy indicators but also from overall inconsistencies. These inconsistencies are between the scales constructed here and virtually all of our control variables and from the low level of correspondence between these scales and the employment and wage policy measure used in Analysis I.

NOTES

1. Beck and Katz (1996) have devised a better method of estimating time-series cross-sectional models. However, their methodology was not in usable form at the time of this analysis.

2. To isolate the possible positive influence of the Catholic variable on the existence of abortion policy, separate Logit regressions were run using a binary dependent variable to measure the presence or absence of abortion policy. None of the independent variables were statistically significant using this dependent variable.

3. There may be a question of validity of the findings due to the lack of data for some time points.

4. The lack of parameter estimates and standard errors for the female heads of government variable during the 1960–1975 period is due to the absence of female heads of government during that period.

5. An interactive variable combining two variables, female head of government and political party in power, was introduced to note its effect on the two separate control variables. The new intervening variable had no effect on either control variable.

6. The political party variable was not significant in four of the regressions. This includes both of the 1976–1994 regressions using the second social policy variable, the regression using the employment variable with the inclusion of Greece, Portugal, and Spain, and the regression using the first social policy variable and the 19-nation/1976–1994 data.

7. The 22-nation/1976–94 and the 19-nation/1960–75 analyses of the first social policy variable and the analysis of the employment policy variable excluding Greece, Portugal, and Spain during 1976–1994 were not significant.

8. Initial examinations of the percentage of female policymakers variable included the variable with no lag, a one-, two-, three- and four-year lag. The female policymakers with the three-year lag variable in the 1976–1994 analysis was statistically significant in the hypothesized

positive direction. However, the same variable was insignificant in the regression using the 1960–1994 data.

9. The time-series results for the other control variables are mixed.

10. Two of the parameter estimates for the percentage of socialists in government are not statistically significant.

Chapter 6 ———————————————————————

Conclusion

The primary question of concern here is whether female policymakers are associated with the advancement of women's issues in the policy realm. The question is central to representation theory as applied to democratic systems, yet there has been surprisingly little research on the topic, and what research has been done has produced limited and often contradictory results. The research design and analysis presented here was intended to avoid many of the limitations and problems evident in previous research so as to provide more conclusive evidence on the substantive topic, and in that regard it has been successful: the findings are robust and positive over time and across a wide range of countries regarding the linkage between the presence of female policymakers and the presence of a variety of issues, in two policy realms, of interest to women. The design, analysis, and results thus provide strong evidence regarding the substantive value of female representation in policy-making positions.

In addition, the research has implications for general research in this area. In this regard, this analysis provides further evidence regarding the difficulties of identifying policies that can be clearly and unambiguously considered "women's issues" over time and across a variety of social and cultural contexts. Previous research frequently has reached apparently contradictory conclusions regarding female policymakers' representation of women's issues because the researchers were looking at very different kinds of policies, many of which the policymakers in question might not have perceived to be of interest to women or provide advances in women's rights. In other cases, the same policies might be perceived very differently and the research outcome again might be apparently contradictory if the same policies are examined during different time frames or in very different cultural contexts.

The problem has plagued research on substantive representation for some time; the analysis presented addresses the issue directly by developing several different variations of women's issue policy realms: one category of employment and wage protection policies and two categories of social policies. The results provide strong support for utilizing multiple policy indicators to represent women's issues, particularly as the results vary depending upon the specific policies in question and the time frame and cultural context under consideration. For example, several findings suggest that the indicator used here to reflect employment and wage protection policies of interest to women may not have been perceived in the same way in a nation's earlier time periods or by all nations uniformly across time. Instead, policies such as equal wage legislation, equal employment policies, divorce reform, and maternity services might in fact have been viewed as means to protect women from the harshness of the workplace (e.g., from long hours or dangerous tasks) or social vicissitudes (e.g., from the financial costs of divorce, pregnancy, or parenthood) rather than as policies to expand the rights of women, at least at some points in time or in certain cultural contexts.

Consequently, as our results suggest, nations with more conservative influences on government and/or more traditional cultural and social norms may support adoption of such policies more strongly than do those countries commonly associated with the advancement of women's rights, or those in the latter category may have supported such policies in an earlier time period, when women's roles were viewed very differently, but backed away from them in later time periods. This possibility would not have been evident or would have been less evident had we utilized only one type of policy as an indicator, or had we examined only a single time period or a narrower range of types of countries. Hence, the analysis demonstrates the value of examining different time frames and a wider array of types of countries while using and refining multiple policy indicators to represent women's interests.

Similarly, this research demonstrates the difficulties inherent in developing valid measures of policy substance that are consistent with the advancement of women's rights. Although the findings demonstrate the basic validity (with the caveats noted previously) of the general policy scales used in Analysis I, the analysis and results of Analysis II suggest that the attempt here to measure the comprehensiveness of equal wage legislation is much more problematic. This measurement problem may be due to the policy components that were chosen to construct the scales or the values associated with the components. Furthermore, the decision to analyze the comprehensiveness of a policy that, in certain nations, is viewed as a method to protect the limitations of women in the labor force may have caused further problems with the analysis. Whatever the reason, the negative results of Analysis II call into question the validity of the measure itself and highlight some of the difficulties of developing valid indicators of policy substance.

In addition, these findings also suggest weaknesses in some of the hypotheses in extant literature. This analysis shows that female heads of government, party dominance, socialist strength, Catholic influence, unions, percentage of women in the labor force or of childbearing age, and the economic level of the nations affect women's policies in a way that is inconsistent and/or contradictory to previous research. Yet, in many such cases, research on allied topics provides support for the results demonstrated here, suggesting the weakness may lie in the original hypothesis rather than in the analysis. This suggests that further analysis regarding these variables, or analysis of policies similar to the ones used here, is needed. Therefore, this study makes substantial contributions and corrections to the extant research on this topic.

The theoretical and substantive implications of this study are clear and compelling. The results show that female representation is associated with employment and social policies that benefit women; the robustness of the findings suggests a strong and consistent relationship between the percentage of female policymakers and policy outputs. Furthermore, because female representation is lagged for four years, the results support the literature that indicates policymakers need some time to learn the system and develop seniority to influence the system.

These findings provide strong support for representation theory, especially theories addressing the link between descriptive and substantive representation. As noted in chapter one, substantive representation concentrates on the activity that happens during representation. Rather than relying on the potential for representation (associated with descriptive representation), the representative's actions and responsibilities provide the explanation for representation. Hence, the representative's dedication to issues that are important to the represented and the outcomes of the representative's actions determine representation.

Although female representatives may initially acquire office due to shared characteristics between the represented and the representative (as found in descriptive representation), it is the subsequent assumption that the representative will act in the best interest of the represented that provides the connection to substantive representation. In this study, it is theorized that female representatives not only share similar characteristics with female constituents but also act on these similarities through their decision making. As a result female policymakers prioritize issues and make decisions that benefit the represented, which in this case refers to female constituents. Though further research is needed to delineate the mechanisms that connect female policymakers with policies, these findings provide strong evidence of a consistent positive connection between the presence of female policymakers and the presence of policies of interest to women.

When we consider these results, it is apparent that further research is needed both to clarify what is meant by women's issue policies and to extend the examination of the female influence on policy making over time and across different nations. Over the last thirty years the number of female representatives has increased throughout the industrialized nations; in this study, the results suggest that this increase has influenced policy outputs. As the opportunity to observe the effect of female representatives on the development of women's issue policies continues, we anticipate that the female influence will also continue. Consequently, as more women hold policy making positions over prolonged time periods, it is expected that the feminine influence will result in the adoption and implementation of more policies of interest to women.

Appendix

Data for tables are taken from different sources and may not be completely compatible.

INDEPENDENT VARIABLES

Female Heads of Government

Source: The World's Women 1970–1995 Trends and Statistics.

Percent Female Union Membership

Sources: OECD Employment Outlook 1991–1992, Paris; OECD Labour Force Statistics: Demographic Trends 1950–1990; Women and the European Labour Markets (1995); *Trade Union Membership* (1985); Australia: Commonwealth Bureau of Census and Statistics, *Labour Report* (various years); Australian Bureau of Statistics, *Labour Statistics* (various years); Austria: Federal Chancellery, *Women in Austria 1985–1995; Labour Market Contracts and Institutions* (1993); Belgium: European Trade Union Confederation (1976); *Trade Unions in Europe* (1974); Canada: Statistics Canada, *Annual Report of the Ministry of Industry, Trade, and Commerce under the Corporations and Labour Unions Returns Act* (1978); Statistics Canada, *Corporations and Labour Unions Returns Act* (various years); *Women and Unions* (1980); Finland: *Women and Trade Unions* (1977); *Statistical Yearbook of Finland* (1964, 1967); Germany: *SJ. GFR* (various years); *Frauen und*

Arbeit (1989); *The Politics of the West German Trade Unions* (1986); International Institute for Labour Studies, *Women and Industrial Relations* (1978); Ireland: *Trade Unions in Europe* (1974); Japan: *Basic Survey of Trade Unions* (1981); *Labour Force Survey* (1980); Netherlands: *Labour Market Contracts and Institutions* (1993); New Zealand: H. Roth, *Trade Unions in New Zealand* (1973); *The Gender Factor* (1992); Norway: *Women and Trade Unions* (1984); Portugal: Commission for Equality and Women's Rights, *Portugal Status of Women* (1991); Sweden: *Trade Unions in the Developed Economies* (1981); United Kingdom: *Department of Employment Gazette* (1979); *British Labour Statistics* (1971); *Gender and Trade Unions* (1994); United States: U.S. Department of Labor, *Directory of National Unions and Employee Associations* (1980); *Accounting for the Decline in Union Membership* (1985).

Percent Females in the Labor Force

Sources: OECD Employment Outlook 1991–1992; U.S. OECD Historical Statistics (various years); *OECD Labour Force Statistics: Demographic Trends 1950–1990*; Bureau of Labor Statistics, *Monthly Labour Review* (1989); Australia: *CBCS Census* (various years); Austria: J. Hartog & J. Theeuwest, eds., *Labour Market Contracts and Institutions* (1993); Canada: Joya Sen, *Women, Unions and the Labour Market* (1994); *Corporations and Labour Unions Returns Act, Canada* (various years); Ireland: *Labour Force Survey* (1979); New Zealand: *All About Women in New Zealand* (1993).

Percent Women of Childbearing Age

Source: U.N. Demographic Yearbook (various years).

DEPENDENT VARIABLES

Employment Policy Variable

Sources: Australia: *Sisters in Suits*; Austria: *Women in Austria 1985–1995*, Federal Chancellery, *Social Security in Austria*; Belgium: *Women of Europe No. 26, The State and the Family*; Canada: *Canada Yearbook*

1994, The State and the Family; Denmark: *Equality in Law Between Men and Women in the EC, The State and the Family*; Finland: FinFo, *Facts about Finland, Act on Equality Between Women and Men*; France: *Women in France*, vol. 95.30; Germany: *Women Workers in Fifteen Countries, Comparative Women's Rights and Political Participation in Europe*; Greece: Women in Decision Making, Greece, *National Report on Greece, The State and the Family*; Iceland: *Women and Equality in Iceland*; Ireland: Childcare and Equal Opportunities, *Comparative Women's Rights and Political Participation in Europe, Working Women*; Italy: *Women Workers in Fifteen Countries, The State and the Family*; Japan: *Women Workers in Fifteen Countries, The State and the Family*; Netherlands: *Women of Europe 1988–92, Equality in Law Between Men and Women in the EC, The State and the Family*; New Zealand: Status of New Zealand Women, *Equal Pay for Women*; Norway: *Comparative Women's Rights and Political Participation in Europe, Unfinished Democracy*; Portugal: Commission for Equality and Women's Rights, *Portugal Status of Women* (1991); Spain: *Equal Opportunities for Women Plan of Action 1988–1990, Comparative Women's Rights and Political Participation in Europe*; Sweden: *Women Workers in Fifteen Countries, Comparative Women's Rights and Political Participation in Europe*; Switzerland: *The Social Structure of Switzerland, Great Achievements—Small Changes? On the Situation of Women in Switzerland*; United Kingdom: *Women Workers in Fifteen Countries, Equal Employment Policy for Women;* United States: *Equal Employment for Women, The Economics of Comparable Worth, Child Care, Parental Leave and the Under 3s.*

Social Policy Variable

Sources: Abortion Policies: *A Global Review*; Australia: *Sisters in Suits*; Austria: *Women in Austria 1985–1995*, Federal Chancellery, *Social Security in Austria*; Belgium: *Women of Europe 1983–87, The State and the Family*; Canada: *Canada Yearbook 1994, Losing Common Ground, The State and the Family*; Denmark: Social Policy in Denmark, *The Danish Government's Report on Physical and Sexual Violence against Women in Denmark, The State and the Family*; Finland: FinFo, *Facts about Finland; Equality, A Habit to Aim For; Violence Against Women in Finland in 1995; Child Care, Parental Leave and the Under 3s*; France: *Women in France*, vol. 95.30, *Women and Politics Worldwide*; Germany: *Women and Politics Worldwide, Comparative State Feminism*; Greece: Women in Decision Making; Greece, *National Report on Greece, The State and the Family*; Iceland: *Women and Equality in Iceland, The European Women's Almanac*; Ireland: *Childcare and Equal Opportunities, Contemporary Western European Feminism*; Italy: *The State and the Family, Western European Feminism*; Japan: *Women of Japan and Korea, The Japanese Woman*; Netherlands: *Women of Europe 1988–92, The State and the Family*; New Zealand: *Status of New Zealand Women*; Norway: *Women and Politics Worldwide, The State and the Family*; Portugal: Commission for Equality and Women's Rights, *Portugal Status of Women* (1991); Spain: *Equal Opportunities for Women Plan of Action 1988–1990, The State and the Family*; Sweden: *Comparative Women's Rights and Political Participation in Europe*; Switzerland: The Social Structure of Switzerland, *Great Achievements—Small Changes? On the Situation of Women in Switzerland*; United Kingdom: *The State and the Family, Comparative Women's Rights and Political Participation in Europe*; United States: *The State and the Family, Child Care, Parental Leave and the Under 3s.*

Bibliography

Addison, J. T. 1975. "Gleichberechtigung—The German Experience." In *Equal Pay for Women*, ed. Barrie O. Pettman. England: MCB Books.

Alvarez, R. Michael, Geoffrey Garrett, & Peter Lange. 1991. "Government Partisanship, Labor Organization, and Macroeconomic Performance." *American Political Science Review* 85:539–56.

Anderson, K. 1975. "Working Women and Political Participation, 1952–72." *American Journal of Political Science* 19:439–53.

Asscher-Vonk, Irene. 1995. *Equality in Law Between Men and Women in the European Community: The Netherlands*. Luxembourg: Office for Official Publications of the European Communities.

Australian Bureau of Statistics. 1977. *Labour Statistics 1975*. Canberra: Australian Bureau of Statistics.

Australian Bureau of Statistics. 1978. *Labour Statistics 1976*. Canberra: Australian Bureau of Statistics.

Ballestrero, Maria V. 1984. "Women at Work in Italy: Legislation-Evolution and Prospects." In *Working Women*, eds. M. Davidson & C. Cooper. Chichester: John Wiley & Sons.

Bashevkin, Sylvia. 1996. "Losing Common Ground." *Canadian Journal of Political Science* 24:225–31.

Baxter, Sandra, & Marjorie Lansing. 1980. *Women and Politics: The Invisible Majority*. Ann Arbor: University of Michigan Press.

Beal, Edwin F., Edward D. Wickersham & Philip K. Kienast. 1976. *The Practice of Collective Bargaining*. Homewood, IL: Richard D. Irwin, Inc.

Beccalli, Bianca. 1985. "Italy." In *Women Workers in Fifteen Countries*, ed. Jennie Farley. New York: ILR Press.

Beck, Nathaniel & Jonathan N. Katz. 1995. "What to Do (and Not to Do) With Time-Series Cross-Sectional Data." *American Political Science Review* 89:634–47.

Beckwith, Karen. 1986. *American Women and Political Participation: The Impacts of Work, Generations, and Feminism.* Westport, CT: Greenwood.

Bennett, Linda & Stephen E. Bennett. 1989. "Enduring Gender Differences in Political Interest: The Impact of Socialization and Political Dispositions." *American Politics Quarterly* 17:105–22.

Berelson, Bernard, Paul Lazarsfeld, & William McPhee. 1954. *Voting.* Chicago: University of Chicago Press.

Berg, John C. 1994. *Unequal Struggle.* Boulder, San Francisco, Oxford: Westview Press.

Berkman, Michael B. & Robert E. O'Connor. 1993. "Do Women Legislators Matter? Female Legislators and State Abortion Policy." *American Politics Quarterly* 21:102–24.

Bernstein, Robert & Jayne Polly. 1975. "Race, Class and Support for Female Candidates." *Western Political Quarterly* 28:733–36.

Beyme, Klaus von. 1985. *Political Parties in Western Democracies.* English translation by Eileen Martin. New York: St. Martin's Press.

Blau, Francine D. & Marianne A. Ferber. 1992. "Women's Work and Women's Lives: A Comparative Economic Perspective." In *Women's Work and Women's Lives*, eds. Hilda Kahne & Janet Z. Giele. Boulder: Westview Press.

Blomquist. Hans C. 1996. "Women in the European Union: Equality Achieved?" In *Economic Development and Women in the World Community*, ed. K. C. Roy, C. A. Tisdell & H. C. Blomquist. Westport, CT: Praeger Publishers.

Bourque, Susan & Jean Grossholtz. 1974. "Politics an Unnatural Practice: Political Science Looks at Female Participation." *Politics and Society* 4:225–66.

British Department of Employment. 1971. *British Labour Statistics.* London: H. M. Stationery Office.

British Department of Employment. 1979. *Department of Employment Gazette.* London: H. M. Stationary Office.

Bullock, Charles, III & Patricia Lee Findley Heys. 1972. "Recruitment of Women for Congress: A Research Note." *Western Political Quarterly* 25: 416–23.

Burnham, Walter Dean. 1982. *The Current Crisis in American Politics*. New York: Oxford University Press.

Burnham, Walter Dean. 1987. "The Turnout Problem." In *Electrons American Style*, ed. A. J. Reichley. Washington, DC: Brookings Institution.

Caldwell, Lesley. "Women, the State, and Italy." Paper presented at the Conference of the PSA Women's Association, October 1982.

Campbell, Angus, Philip Converse, Warren Miller, & Donald Stokes. 1960. *The American Voter*. New York: Wiley.

Carmo Nunes, Maria de. 1984. "Women at Work in Portugal." In *Working Women*, ed. M. Davidson & C. Cooper. Chichester: John Wiley & Sons.

Carroll, Berenice A. 1979. "Political Science, Part I: American Politics and Political Behavior." *Signs* 5:289–306.

Castles, Francis. 1981. "Female Legislative Representation and the Electoral System." *Politics* 1:21–26.

Castles, Francis G. 1982. "The Impact of Parties on Public Expenditure." In *The Impact of Parties*, ed. F. Castles. London: Sage Publications, Ltd.

Cayer, N. Joseph & Lee Sigelman. 1980. "Minorities and Women in State and Local Government: 1973–1975." *Public Administration Review* 40:443–50.

Center for the American Woman and Politics. *Women in Elective Office Fact Sheet*. 1990, 1991, and 1993. New Brunswick, NJ: CAWP, Eagleton Institute of Politics, Rutgers University.

Chiplin, Brian & Peter Sloan. 1976. *Sex Discrimination in the Labour Market*. London: Macmillan.

Cole, Leonard A. 1976. *Blacks in Power: A Comparative Study of Black and White Elected Officials*. Princeton: Princeton University Press.

Collins, Helen. 1992. *The Equal Opportunities Handbook*. Oxford: Blackwell Publishers.

Commission of the European Communities. 1976. *European Trade Union Confederation*. Brussels: Trade Union Division of the Directorate-General for Information; Washington, DC: European Communities Information.

Commonwealth Bureau of Census and Statistics. 1966. *Census Data*

on the Total Australian Population. Canberra: Commonwealth
Bureau of Census and Statistics.

Commonwealth Bureau of Census and Statistics. 1971. *Census Data
on the Total Australian Population*. Canberra: Commonwealth
Bureau of Census and Statistics.

Commonwealth Bureau of Census and Statistics. 1972. *Labour Report,
no. 57*. Canberra: Commonwealth Bureau of Census and Statistics.

Commonwealth Bureau of Census and Statistics. 1973. *Labour Report,
no. 58*. Canberra: Commonwealth Bureau of Census and Statistics.

Commonwealth Bureau of Census and Statistics. 1976. *Census Data
on the Total Australian Population*. Canberra: Commonwealth
Bureau of Census and Statistics.

Conover, Pamela Johnston. 1988. "Feminists and the Gender Gap."
Journal of Politics 50:985–1010.

Conyers, James E. & Walter L. Wallace. 1976. *Black Elected Officials:
A Study of Black Americans Holding Governmental Office*. New
York: Russell Sage Foundation.

Cook, Alice H. 1980. "Women in Trade Unions." In *Women and Industrial Relations*, research series no. 56. Geneva: International
Institute for Labour Studies.

Cotton, Jeremiah. 1988. "On the Decomposition of Wage Differentials." *Review of Economics and Statistics* 70:236–43.

Dahlerup, Drude. 1988. "From a Small to a Large Minority: Women
in Scandinavian Politics." *Scandinavian Political Studies* 11:
275–98.

Darcy, R., Susan Welch & Janet Clark. 1987. *Women, Elections &
Representation*. New York: Longman, Inc.

Davidson, R. H. 1967. "Congress and the Executive: The Race for Representation." In *Congress: The First Branch of Government*, ed.
A. DeGrazia. New York: Anchor.

Davidson, Roger H. & Walter J. Oleszek. 1994. *Congress and Its Members*. Washington, DC: Congressional Quarterly, Inc.

de Rijik, Tineki. 1984. "Women at Work in Holland." In *Working
Women*, ed. M. Davidson & C. Cooper. Chichester: John Wiley
& Sons.

Diamond, Irene. 1977. *Sex Roles in the State House*. New Haven: Yale
University Press.

Diamond, Irene & Nancy Hartsock. 1981. "Beyond Interests in Politics: A Comment on Virginia Sapiro's 'When Are Interests Interesting? The Problem of Political Representation of Women.'" *American Political Science Review* 75:717–21.

Dickens, William T. & Jonathan S. Leonard. 1985. "Accounting for the Decline in Union Membership." *Industrial and Labor Relations Review* 38:3.

Dodson, Debra L. 1989. "A Comparison of the Impact of Women's and Men's Attitudes on Their Legislative Behavior: Is What They Say What They Do?" Paper presented at the Annual Meeting of the American Political Science Association Meeting, San Francisco, CA, 1989.

Doring, Herbert. 1995. *Parliaments and Majority Rule in Western Europe*. New York: St. Martin's Press.

Dresang, D. L. 1974. "Ethnic Politics, Representative Bureaucracy, and Development Administration: The Zambian Case." *American Political Science Review* 68:1605–17.

Duverger, Maurice. 1955. *The Political Role of Women*. Paris: UNESCO.

Dye, Thomas R. 1966. *Politics, Economics, and the Public Outcomes in the American States*. Chicago: Rand McNally.

Dye, Thomas R. 1976. *Policy Analysis*. Tuscaloosa: University of Alabama Press.

Dye, Thomas R. 1979. "Politics Versus Economics: The Development of the Literature on Policy Determination." *Policy Studies Journal* 7:652–62.

Dye, Thomas R. & James Renick. 1981. "Political Power and City Jobs: Determinants of Minority Employment." *Social Science Quarterly* 62:457–86.

Eduards, Maud, Geatrice Halsaa & Hege Skjeie. 1985. "Equality: How Equal?" In *Unfinished Democracy*, ed. E. Haavio-Mannila et al. Oxford, NY: Pergamon Press.

Eisinger, P. 1982. "Black Employment in Municipal Jobs: The Impact of Black Political Power." *American Political Science Review* 76:380–92.

England, Paula. 1992. *Comparable Worth: Theories and Evidence*. New York: Walter de Gruyter, Inc.

England, Paula & Bahar Norris. 1985. "Comparable Worth: A New

Doctrine of Sex Discrimination." *Social Science Quarterly* 66: 629–43.

Equal Status Council of Iceland. 1992. *Women and Equality in Iceland.* Reykjavik, Iceland: Equal Status Council of Iceland.

Ericsson, Ylva. 1985. "Sweden." In *Women Workers in Fifteen Countries*, ed. J. Farley. New York: Cornell University Press.

Erikson, Robert & Norman Luttbeg. 1973. *American Public Opinion: Its Origins, Content, and Impact.* New York: Wiley.

Eskola, Matti, ed. 1994. *Facts About Finland.* Helsinki: Otava Publishing Company Ltd.

Eulau, Heinz & Paul Karps. 1977. "The Puzzle of Representation: Specifying Components of Responsiveness." *Legislative Studies Quarterly* 2, no. 3:233–54.

Eulau, Heinz & Kenneth Prewitt. 1973. *Labyrinths of Democracy: Adaptations, Linkages, Representation, and Policies in Urban Politics.* Indianapolis: Bobbs-Merrill.

Farley, Jennie, ed. 1985. *Women Workers in Fifteen Countries.* Ithaca, New York: International Industrial and Labor Relations Press.

Federal Statistical Office/Federal Republic of Germany. 1964. *SJ, GFR: Statistisches Jahrbuch.* Wiesbaden: Metzler-Poeschel.

Federal Statistical Office/Federal Republic of Germany. 1971. *SJ, GFR: Statistisches Jahrbuch.* Wiesbaden: Metzler-Poeschel.

Federal Statistical Office/Federal Republic of Germany. 1976. *SJ, GFR: Statistisches Jahrbuch.* Wiesbaden: Metzler-Poeschel.

Federal Statistical Office/Federal Republic of Germany. 1981. *SJ, GFR: Statistisches Jahrbuch.* Wiesbaden: Metzler-Poeschel.

Feigl, Susanne. 1995. *Women in Austria 1985–1995.* Vienna: Federal Chancellery.

Fenno, Richard F. 1987. "Congressmen and Committees: A Comparative Analysis." In *Congress: Structure and Policy*, eds. M. McCubbins & T. Sullivan. Cambridge: Cambridge University Press.

Fernandez, Matilde Vazquez. 1993. "Spain." In *European Women in Business and Management*, eds. Marilyn J. Davidson & Cary L. Cooper. London: Paul Chapman Publishing, Ltd.

Ferree, M. M. 1974. "A Women for President: Changing Responses, 1958–1972." *Public Opinion Quarterly* 38:390–99.

Figes, Eva. 1970. *Patriarchal Attitudes.* Greenwich, CT: Fawcett Publications.

Flanz, Gisbert H. 1983. *Comparative Women's Rights and Political Participation in Europe*. New York: Transnational Publishers, Inc.

Fraga, Luis R., Kenneth J. Meier & Robert E. England. 1986. "Hispanic Americans and Educational Policy: Limits to Equal Access." *Journal of Politics* 48:850–76.

Frankovic, Kathleen A. 1977. "Sex and Voting in the U.S. House of Representatives, 1961–1975." *American Politics Quarterly* 5: 315–31.

Frankovic, Kathleen A. 1982. "Sex and Politics—New Alignments, Old Issues." *PS: Political Science and Politics* 15:439–48.

French Embassy. 1995. *Women in France, Vol. 95.30*. Washington, D.C.: French Embassy Press and Information Service.

Friedland, Roger & Jimmy Sanders. 1985. "The Public Economy and Economic Growth in Western Market Economies." *American Sociological Review* 50:421–37.

Gaudart, Dorothea & Rose Marie Greve. 1978. *Women and Industrial Relations*. Geneva: International Institute for Labour Studies.

Gauthier, Anne Helene. 1996. *The State and the Family*. Oxford: Clarendon Press.

Gehlen, Freida. 1977. "Women Members of Congress: A Distinctive Role." In *A Portrait of Marginality*, eds. M. Githens & J. L. Prestage. New York: Longman Group Ltd.

Gelb, Joyce & Marian Lief Palley, eds. 1994. *Women of Japan and Korea*. Philadelphia: Temple University Press.

Gertzog. Irwin N. 1995. *Congressional Women*. Westport, CT: Praeger Publishers.

Githens, Marianne. 1994. "Political Issues." In *Different Roles, Different Voices*, ed. M. Githens, P. Norris & J. Lovenduski. New York: Harper Collins College Publishers.

Gormley, William, John Hoadley & Charles Williams. 1983. "Potential Responsiveness in the Bureaucracy: Views of Public Utility Regulation." *American Political Science Review* 77:704–17.

Goul Andersen, J. 1984. *Women and Politics*. Aarhus, Denmark: Forlaget Politica.

Greenberger, Marcia. 1980. "The Effectiveness of Federal Laws Prohibiting Sex Discrimination in Employment in the United States." In *Equal Employment Policy for Women*, ed. R. Steinberg Ratner. Philadelphia: Temple University Press.

Gunderson, Morley. 1975. "Equal Pay in Canada: History, Progress, and Problems." In *Equal Pay for Women*, ed. Barrie O. Pettman. England: MCB Books.

Gurin, Patricia. 1987. "The Political Implications of Women's Statuses." In *Spouse, Parent, Worker*, ed. F. J. Crosby. New Haven: Yale University Press.

Haavind, Hanne. 1982. "Premisser for Personlige Forhold Mellom Kvinner (Premises for Personal Relations Between Women)." In *Kvinner i Felleskap (Women Together)*, ed. H. Holter. Oslo: Universitetsforlaget.

Haavio-Mannila, E., et al. 1985. *Unfinished Democracy: Women in Nordic Politics*. London & New York: Pergamon Press.

Haines, Janine. 1992. *Suffrage to Sufferance*. New South Wales, Australia: Allen & Unwin.

Hansen, Susan B. 1995. "Was Susan B. Anthony Wrong? State Public Policy and the Representation of Women's Interests." Paper presented at the Annual Meeting of the American Political Science Association, Chicago, IL, 1995.

Hayashi, Hiroko. 1985. "Japan." In *Women Workers in Fifteen Countries*, ed. Jennie Farley. New York: ILR Press.

Heidenheimer, Arnold J., Hugh Heclo & Carolyn Teich Adams. 1990. *Comparative Public Policy*. New York: St. Martin's Press.

Hellenic Republic. 1995. *National Report on Greece*. Athens: National Printing House.

Hewitt, C. 1977. "The Effect of Political Democracy and Social Democracy on Equality in Industrial Societies: A Cross-National Comparison." *American Sociological Review* 42.

Heywood, John S. & George Nezlek. 1993. "The Gender Wage Gap Among Software Workers: Trends Over the Last Two Decades." *Social Science Quarterly* 74:603–13.

Hibbs, Douglas A. 1977. "Political Parties and Macroeconomic Policy." *American Political Science Review* 71:1467–87.

Hicks, Alexander. 1994. "Introduction to Pooling." In *The Comparative Political Economy of the Welfare State*, ed. T. Janooski & A. Hicks. New York: Cambridge University Press.

Hicks, Alexander & Duane Swank. 1992. "Politics, Institutions, and Welfare Spending in Industrialized Democracies, 1960–1982." *American Political Science Review* 86: 658–74.

Hill, Kim Quaile & Jan E. Leighley. 1992. "The Policy Consequences of Class Bias in State Electorates." *American Journal of Political Science* 36:351–65.

Huddy, Leonie & Nayda Terkildsen. 1993. "Gender Stereotypes and the Perception of Male and Female Candidates." *American Journal of Political Science* 37:119–47.

Inglehart, M. 1981. "Political Interest in West European Women: An Historical and Empirical Comparative Analysis." *Comparative Political Studies* 14:299–326.

Instituto de la Mujer. 1991. *Equal Opportunities for Women: Plan of Action 1988–1990.* Madrid: Ministerio de Asuntos Sociales.

International Labor Organization. 1965–1995. *Yearbook of Labor Statistics.* Geneva, Switzerland: International Labour Office.

International Labor Organization. 1987. *World Labour Report.* New York: Oxford University Press.

International Workshop for Labour Market Contracts and Institutions. 1993. *Labour Market Contracts and Institutions.* Amsterdam; New York: North Holland.

Iwao, Sumiko. 1993. *The Japanese Woman.* New York: The Free Press.

Jackman, Robert W. 1980. "Socialist Parties and Income Inequalities in Western Industrial Societies." *Journal of Politics* 42: 135–49.

Jacobson, Gary C. 1990. *The Politics of Congressional Elections.* Boston: Little, Brown and Company.

Japan. 1980. *Labor Force Survey.* Tokyo: Sorifu Tokeikyoku.

Japan. 1981. *Basic Survey of Trade Unions.* Tokyo: Labor Ministry.

Jaquette, Jane S. 1974. "Introduction." In *Women in Politics*, ed. J. Jaquette. New York: Wiley.

Jennings, M. Kent & Richard G. Niemi. 1981. *Generations and Politics: A Panel Study of Young Adults and Their Parents.* Princeton: Princeton University Press.

Jenson, Jane. 1995. "Extending the Boundaries of Citizenship: Women's Movements of Western Europe." In *The Challenge of Local Feminisms*, ed. A. Basu. Boulder, Colorado: Westview Press.

Jenson, Jane & Mariette Sineau. 1994. "France." In *Women and Politics Worldwide.* New Haven: Yale University Press.

Jonasdöttir, Anna G. 1988. "On the Concept of Interest, Women's Interest, and the Limitations of Interest Theory." In *The Political*

Interests of Gender, eds. K. Jones & A. Jonasdóttir. London: Sage Publications, Ltd.

Kamerman, Sheila B. & Alfred J. Kahn. 1991. "A U.S. Policy Challenge." In *Child Care, Parental Leave, and the Under 3s*, ed. S. Kamerman & A. Kahn. Westport, CT: Auburn House.

Kaplan, Gisela. 1992. *Contemporary Western European Feminism*. Sydney, Australia: Allen & Unwin.

Karnig, A. 1975. "Private-regarding Policy, Civil Rights Groups, and the Mediating Impact of Municipal Reforms." *American Journal of Political Science* 19:91–106.

Karnig. A. 1976. "Black Representation on City Councils." *Urban Affairs Quarterly* 12:223–42.

Karvonen, Lauri & Per Selle. 1995. "Introduction: Scandinavia: A Case Apart." In *Women in Nordic Politics*, ed. L. Karvonen & P. Selle. England: Dartmouth Publishing Company, Ltd.

Keefe, William & Morris Ogul. 1997. *The American Legislative Process*. Englewood Cliffs, N.J: Prentice-Hall.

Kelber, Mim. 1994. *Women and Government*. Westport, CT: Praeger.

Keller, E. 1978. "The Impact of Black Mayors on Urban Policy." *The Annals* 439:40–52.

Kelly, Rita Mae, Michelle A. Saint-German & Jody D. Horn. 1991. "Female Public Officials: A Different Voice?" In *The Annals of the American Academy of Political and Social Science*, ed. Janet K. Boles. Newbury Park, CA: Sage Publications.

Keman, Hans. 1982. "Securing the Safety of the Nation-State." In *The Impact of Parties*, ed. F. G. Castles. London: Sage Publications.

Killingsworth, Mark R. 1990. *The Economics of Comparable Worth*. Kalamazoo: W. E. Upjohn Institute for Employment Research.

King, A. 1981. "What Do Elections Decide?" In *Democracy at the Polls*, eds. D. Butler, H. R. Penniman & A. Ranney. Washington, DC: AEI.

Kirkpatrick, Jeane. 1974. *Political Woman*. New York: Basic Books.

Kohl, Jürgen. 1981. "Trends and Problems in Postwar Public Expenditure Development in Western Europe and North America." In *The Development of Welfare States in Europe and America*, eds. P. Flora & A. Heidenheimer. New Brunswick, NJ: Transaction Books.

Koole, Ruud & Peter Mair, eds. 1992. "Special Issue: Political Data Yearbook, 1992." *European Journal of Political Research* 22, no. 4.

Laissy, Ana Paula, ed. 1982. *Women of Europe*. Brussels, Belgium: Commission of the European Communities. No. 26.

Laissy, Ana Paula, ed. 1983–1984. *Women of Europe*. Brussels, Belgium: Commission of the European Communities. Nos. 33 & 34.

Laissy, Ana Paula, ed. 1988. *Women of Europe 1983–1987*. Brussels, Belgium: Commission of the European Communities.

Laissy, Ana Paula, ed. 1993. *Women of Europe 1988–1992*. Brussels, Belgium: Commission of the European Communities.

Lane, Jan-Erik, David McKay & Kenneth Newton. 1991. *Political Data Handbook*. Oxford: Oxford University Press.

Langer, Ingrid. 1989. *Frauen und Arbeit*. Frankfurt am Main: dipa-Verlag.

Lawrence, Elizabeth. 1994. *Gender and Trade Unions*. London: Taylor & Francis Ltd.

Leader, Shelah Gilbert. 1977. "The Policy Impact of Elected Women Officials." In *The Impact of the Electoral Process*, eds. Louis Maisel & Joseph Cooper. Beverly Hills: Sage Publications.

Leeper, Mark S. 1991. "The Impact of Prejudice on Female Candidates: An Experimental Look at Voter Inference." *American Politics Quarterly* 19:248–61.

Leijon, Anna-Greta. 1975. "Sexual Equality in the Labour Market." *International Labour Review* 112:109–23.

Lemke, Christiane. 1994. "Women and Politics: The New Federal Republic of Germany." In *Women and Politics Worldwide*, ed. B. Nelson & N. Chowdhury. New Haven: Yale University Press.

Levy, Rene. 1984. *The Social Structure of Switzerland*. Zurich: Pro Helvetia Division Documentation Press.

Lewenhak, Sheila. 1977. *Women and Trade Unions*. New York: St. Martin's Press.

Loree, Marguerite J. 1980. "Equal Pay and Equal Opportunity Law in France." In *Equal Employment Policy for Women*, ed. R. Steinberg Ratner. Philadelphia: Temple University Press.

Louekari, Maarit. 1995. *Finfo, Social Welfare*. Helsinki: Ministry for Foreign Affairs, Department for Press and Culture.

Lovenduski, Joni. 1986. *Women and European Politics*. Brighton, Sussex: Wheatsheaf Books.

Lovenduski, Joni, 1993. "Introduction: The Dynamics of Gender and Party." In *Gender and Party Politics*, ed. J. Lovenduski & P. Norris. London: Sage Publication.

Lovenduski, Joni & Jill Hills. 1981. *The Politics of the Second Electorate*. London: Routledge and Kegan Paul.

Luttbeg, N. 1974. *Public Opinion and Public Policy*. Homewood, IL: Dorsey Press.

MacLennan, Emma & Nickie Fonda. 1985. "Great Britain." In *Women Workers in Fifteen Countries*, ed. Jennie Farley. New York: Cornell University Press.

Mahowald, Mary. 1978. *Philosophy of Women: Classical to Current Concepts*. Indianapolis: Hackett.

Makward, Christiane. 1975. "French Women In Politics, 1975." *Michigan Papers in Women's Studies* 1:123–28.

Mandel, Ruth B. 1981. *In the Running*. New York: Ticknor and Fields.

Markovits, Andrei S. 1986. *The Politics of the West German Trade Unions*. Cambridge: Cambridge University Press.

Marks, Gary W. 1989. *Unions in Politics*. Princeton: Princeton University Press.

Marsden, Lorna R. 1980. "The Role of the National Action Committee on the Status of Women in Facilitating Equal Pay Policy in Canada." In *Equal Employment Policy for Women*, ed. Ronnie Steinberg Ratner. Philadelphia: Temple University Press.

Martin, Janet. 1989. "The Recruitment of Women to Cabinet and Subcabinet Posts." *Western Political Quarterly* 42:161–72.

Mazur, Amy G. 1995. "Strong State and Symbolic Reform: The Ministere des Droits de la Femme in France." In *Comparative State Feminism*, ed. Dorothy McBride Stetson & Amy G. Mazur. Thousand Oaks: Sage Publications.

McKenna, Anne. 1988. *Childcare and Equal Opportunities*. Dublin: Employment Equality Agency.

Meier, K. J. & G. Nigro. 1976. "Representative Bureaucracy and Policy Preferences: A Study in the Attitudes of Federal Executives." *Public Administration Review* 36:458–69.

Merritt, Sharyne. 1980. "Recruitment of Women to Suburban City Councils: Higgins vs. Chevalier." In *Women in Local Politics*, ed. Debra W. Stewart. Metuchen, NJ & London: The Scarecrow Press.

Mezey, Susan Gluck. 1978. "Does Sex Make a Difference? A Case Study of Women in Politics." *The Western Political Quarterly* 31:492–501.

Mezey, Susan Gluck. 1980. "The Effects of Sex on Recruitment: Connecticut Local Offices." In *Women in Local Politics*, ed. Debra W. Stewart. Metuchen & London: The Scarecrow Press.

Mikkola, Matti. 1991. "Finland: Supporting Parental Choice." In *Child Care, Parental Leave, and the Under 3s*, ed. S. Kammerman & A. Kahn. Westport, CT: Auburn House.

Miliori, Polly. 1993. "Women in Business and Management in Greece." In *European Women in Business and Management*, ed. M. Davidson & C. Cooper. London: Paul Chapman Publishing, Ltd.

Miller, P. W. 1987. "The Wage Effect of the Occupational Segregation of Women in Britain." *Economic Journal* 97:679–99.

Miller, Warren E. & Donald E. Stokes. 1963. "Constituency Influence in Congress." *American Political Science Review* 57:45–56.

Ministry of Labour (Denmark). 1993. *The Danish Government's Report on Physical and Sexual Violence Against Women in Denmark*. Copenhagen: Ministry of Labour.

Ministry for Social Affairs and Health (Finland). 1995. *Act on Equality Between Women and Men*. Helsinki: Publications on Equality.

Ministry for Social Affairs and Health (Finland). 1995. *Violence Against Women in Finland in 1995*. Helsinki: Publications on Equality.

Ministry for Social Affairs and Health (Finland). 1996. *Equality, A Habit to Aim For*. Helsinki: Publications on Equality.

Ministry of Social Affairs. 1995. *Social Policy in Denmark*. Copenhagen: Ry Bogtrykkeri Printing.

Ministry of Women's Affairs. 1992. *Status of New Zealand Women*. Wellington, N.Z.: Ministry of Women's Affairs.

Moussourou, Loukia & Sophia Spiliotopoulos. 1984. "Women at Work in Greece: The Sociological and Legal Perspectives." In *Working Women*, eds. M. Davidson & C. Cooper. Chichester: John Wiley & Sons.

Murdoch, Henry. 1984. "Women at Work in Ireland." In *Working Women*, eds. M. Davidson & C. Cooper. Chichester: John Wiley & Sons.

Murphy, Yvonne. 1993. "Women in Business and Management in Ireland." In *European Women in Business and Management*, ed. M. Davidson & C. Cooper. London: Paul Chapman Publishing, Ltd.

Nielsen, Ruth. 1995. *Equality in Law Between Men and Women in the*

European Community. Luxembourg: Office for Official Publications of the European Communities.

Nieuwenhuysen, John & John Hicks. 1975. "Equal Pay for Women in Australia and New Zealand." In *Equal Pay for Women*, ed. Barrie O. Pettman. England: MCB Ltd.

Norderval, Ingunn. 1985. "Party and Legislative Participation Among Scandinavian Women." In *Women and Politics in Western Europe*, ed. Sylvia Bashevkin. London: Frank Cass & Co. Ltd.

Norris, Pippa. 1985. "The Gender Gap in Britain and America." *Parliamentary Affairs* 38:192–201.

Norris, Pippa. 1987. *Politics and Sexual Equality: The Comparative Position of Women in Western Democracies*. Boulder; Rienner; Brighton, Sussex: Wheatsheaf Books.

Norris, Pippa & Joni Lovenduski. 1989. "Women Candidates for Parliament: Transforming the Agenda?" *British Journal of Political Science* 19, 1:106–15.

Norton, Noelle. 1995. "Committee Position Makes a Difference: Institutional Structure and Women Policy Makers." In *Gender Power, Leadership, and Governance*, ed. G. Duerst-Lahti & R. M. Kelly. Ann Arbor: University of Michigan Press.

OCED. 1983. *Historical Statistics*. Paris: Organization for Economics Cooperation and Development Statistics Directorate; Washington, DC: OECD Washington Center.

OECD. 1987. *Historical Statistics*. Paris: Organization for Economic Cooperation and Development Statistics Directorate; Washington, DC: OECD Washington Center.

OECD. 1988. "Equal Pay for Equal Work." In *OECD Employment Outlook*. Paris: OECD Washington Center.

OECD. 1988. *Quarterly National Accounts*. Paris: Organization for Economic Cooperation and Development Statistics Directorate; Washington, DC: OECD Washington Center.

OECD. 1991. *Labour Force Statistics: Demographic Trends 1950–1990*. Paris: Organization for Economic Cooperation and Development Statistics Directorate; Washington, DC: OECD Washington Center.

OECD. 1992. *Employment Outlook 1991–1992*. Paris: Organization for Economic Cooperation and Development Statistics Directorate; Washington, DC: OECD Washington Center.

OECD. 1996. *Quarterly National Accounts*. Paris: Organization for

Economic Cooperation and Development Statistics Directorate; Washington, DC: OECD Washington Center.

OECD. 1997. *Main Economic Indicators*. Paris: Organization for Economic Cooperation and Development Statistics Directorate; Washington, DC: OECD Washington Center.

Offe, Claus. 1982. *Structural Problems of the Capitalist State*. London: Macmillan.

Olsson, Suzann. 1992. *The Gender Factor*. Palmerston North, N.Z.: Dunmore Press.

O'Neill, June. 1990. "The Decline in the Gender Gap in the 1980s: Some Preliminary Findings for the United States." New York: City University of New York, Baruch College.

Pampel, Fred. 1993. "Relative Cohort Size and Fertility: The Sociopolitical Context of the Easterlin Effect." *American Sociological Review* 58:496–514.

Parenti, Michael. 1970. "Power and Pluralism: The View from the Bottom." *Journal of Politics* 32:501–30.

Parkin, F. 1971. *Class Inequality and Political Order*. London: MacGibbon & Kee.

Pateman, Carole. 1980. "Women and Consent." *Political Theory* 8: 149–68.

Pitkin, Hanna. 1967. *The Concept of Representation*. Berkeley: University of California Press.

Piven, Frances Fox & Richard A. Cloward. 1989. *Why Americans Don't Vote*. New York: Pantheon.

Political Handbook of the World. 1970–1991. New York: McGraw-Hill Book Co.

Prewitt, Kenneth & Alan Stone. 1973. *The Ruling Elites: Elite Theory, Power, and American Democracy*. New York: Harper & Row Publishers.

Ratner, Ronnie Steinberg, ed. 1980. *Equal Employment Policy for Women*. Philadelphia: Temple University Press.

Reingold, Beth. 1990. "Representing Women: A Comparison of Female and Male Legislators in California and Arizona." Paper presented at the Annual Meeting of the American Political Science Association, San Francisco, CA, 1990.

Reingold, Beth. 1992. "Concepts of Representation Among Female and Male State Legislators." *Legislative Studies Quarterly* 17: 509–37.

Reynolds de Sousa, Maria & Dina Canco. 1991. *Portugal Status of Women, Commission for Equality and Women's Rights*. Lisbon: Commission for Equality and Women's Rights, Prime Minister's Office.

Ries, Paula & Anne J. Stone. 1992. *The American Woman 1992–1993*. New York: W. W. Norton & Company, Inc.

Rose, Richard. 1984. *Understanding Big Government: The Programme Approach*. London: Sage Publications.

Roth, Herbert Otto. 1973. *Trade Unions in New Zealand*. Wellington: A. H. & A. W. Reed Ltd.

Rudolf, Gert. 1994. *Social Security in Austria*. Vienna: Federal Press Service.

Rule, Wilma. 1981. "Why Women Don't Run: The Critical Contextual Factors in Women's Legislative Recruitment." *Western Political Quarterly* 34: 60–77.

Rule, Wilma. 1987. "Electoral Systems, Contextual Factors, and Women's Opportunity for Election to Parliament in 23 Democracies." *Western Political Quarterly* 40: 477–98.

Rule, Wilma & Pippa Norris. 1992. "Anglo and Minority Women's Underrepresentation in the Congress: Is the Electoral System the Culprit?" In *The Impact of U.S. Electoral Systems on Minorities and Women*, eds. J. Zimmerman & W. Rule. Westport, CT: Greenwood Press.

Sainsbury, Diane. 1988. "The Scandinavian Model and Women's Interests: The Issues of Universalism and Corporatism." *Scandinavian Political Studies* 11:337–46.

Saint-Germain, Michelle A. 1989. "Does Their Difference Make a Difference? The Impact of Women on Public Policy in the Arizona Legislature." *Social Science Quarterly* 70:956–68.

Saltzstein, Grace Hall. 1986. "Female Mayors and Women in Municipal Jobs." *American Journal of Political Science* 30:140–64.

Saltzstein, Grace Hall. 1989. "Black Mayors and Police Policies." *Journal of Politics* 51, 3:525–44.

Sanzone, Donna. 1984. "Women in Positions of Political Leadership in Britain, France, and West Germany." In *Women and the Public Sphere*. ed. Janet Siltanen & Michelle Stanworth. New York: St. Martin's Press.

Sapiro, Virginia. 1981. "Research Frontier Essay: When Are Interests

Interesting? The Problem of Political Representation of Women." *American Political Science Review* 75:701–16.

Sapiro, Virginia. 1983. *The Political Integration of Women: Roles, Socialization, and Politics*. Urbana-Champaign: University of Illinois.

Sawer, Marian. 1990. *Sisters in Suits: Women in Public Policy in Australia*. Boston: Allen & Unwin Publishing.

Schneider, David M. & Raymond T. Smith. 1973. *Class Differences and Sex Roles in American Kinship and Family Structure*. Englewood Cliffs: Prentice-Hall.

Schopp-Schilling, Hanna Beate. 1985. "Federal Republic of Germany." In *Women Workers in Fifteen Countries*, ed. Jennie Farley. New York: ILR Press.

Schumaker, P. & B. Loomis. 1979. "Responsiveness to Citizen Preference and Societal Problems in American Communities." In *South Atlantic Urban Studies Annual* 3:38–66, ed. S. M. Hines & G. W. Hopkins. Columbia: University of South Carolina Press.

Sen, Joya. 1994. *Women, Unions and the Labour Market*. Acton, MA: Copley Publishing Group.

Shapiro, Robert Y. & Harpreet Mahajan. 1986. "Gender Differences in Policy Preferences: A Summary of Trends from the 1960s to the 1980s." *Public Opinion Quarterly* 50:42–61.

Siebert, W. S. & P. J. Sloane. 1981. "The Measurement of Sex and Marital Status Discrimination at the Workplace." *Economica* 48:125–41.

Sigelman, Lee & Carol K. Sigelman. 1982. "Sexism, Racism, and Ageism in Voting Behavior: An Experimental Analysis." *Social Psychology Quarterly* 45:263–69.

Sinkkonen, Sirkka & Elina Haavio-Mannila. 1981. "The Impact of the Women's Movement and Legislative Activity of Women MPs on Social Development." In *Women, Power, and Political Systems*, ed. Margherita Rendel. London: Croom Helm.

Skard, Torild. 1980. *Utvalgt til Stortinget*. Oslo: Gyldendal.

Skard, Torild & Elina Haavio-Mannila. 1984. "Equality Between the Sexes: Myth or Reality in Norden?" *Daedalus* 113:141–67.

Skjeie, H. 1993. "Malrettet og Tilfeldig: Kvoteringspraksis of Kvinnerepresentasjon pa Stortinget." *Tidskrift For Samfunnsforskning*. 34:479–86.

Smith, E. Owen. 1981. *Trade Unions in the Developed Economies.* New York: St. Martin's Press.

Smith, James P. & Michael P. Ward. 1984. *Women's Wages and Work in the Twentieth Century.* Santa Monica: Rand Corporation.

Snyder, Paula. 1992. *European Women's Almanac.* New York: Colombia University Press.

Sorensen, Elaine. 1991. "Gender and Racial Pay Gaps in the 1980s: Accounting for Different Trends." Urban Institute Research Paper no. 4591, U.S. Dept of Labor Women's Bureau. Washington, DC: Urban Institute.

Stanley, David J., Dean E. Mann & Jameson W. Doig. 1967. *Men Who Govern.* Washington, DC: The Brookings Institution.

Statistical Office of European Communities. 1979. *Labor Force Survey.* Luxembourg: Office for Official Publications of the European Communities.

Statistical Yearbook of Finland. 1964. Helsinki: Tilastokekus.

Statistical Yearbook of Finland. 1967. Helsinki: Tilastokekus.

Statistics Canada. 1976. *Corporations and Labour Unions Returns Act.* Ottawa: Statistics Canada.

Statistics Canada. 1978. *Annual Report of the Ministry of Industry, Trade and Commerce under the Corporations and Labour Unions Returns Act.* Ottawa: Statistics Canada.

Statistics Canada. 1981. *Corporations and Labour Unions Returns Act.* Ottawa: Statistics Canada.

Statistics Canada. 1993. *Canada Yearbook 1994.* Ottawa: Census and Statistics Office.

Statistics New Zealand. 1993. *All About Women in New Zealand.* Wellington, N.Z.: Statistics New Zealand.

Stein, Lana. 1986. "Representative Local Government: Minorities in the Municipal Workforce." *Journal of Politics* 48:694–713.

Stephens, John D. 1986. *The Transition from Capitalism to Socialism.* Urbana & Chicago: University of Illinois Press.

Stetson, Dorothy. 1987. *Women's Rights in France.* Westport, CT: Greenwood Press.

Stewart, Margaret. 1974. *Trade Unions in Europe.* Essex: Gower Press Ltd.

Studer, Liliane (editor). 1995. *Great Achievements-Small Changes? On the Situation of Women in Switzerland.* Translation by Jacqueline Gartmann. Berne: Federal Commission for Women's Issues.

Takahashi, Nobuko. 1976. "Women's Wages in Japan and the Question of Equal Pay." In *Women Workers and Society*. Geneva: International Labour Organization.

Thomas, Sue. 1989. "Voting Patterns in the California Assembly: The Role of Gender." *Women and Politics* 9:43–53.

Thomas, Sue. 1991a. "The Impact of Women on State Legislative Policies." *Journal of Politics* 53:958–76.

Thomas, Sue 1991b. "The Effects of Race and Gender on Constituency Service." *The Western Political Quarterly* 45:169–80.

Thomas, Sue. 1992. "When Women Legislate." Paper presented at the Western Political Science Association Annual Meeting, San Francisco, CA, March 1992.

Thomas, Sue. 1994. *How Women Legislate*. New York & Oxford: Oxford University Press.

Thomas, Sue & Susan Welch. 1991. "The Impact of Gender on Activities and Priorities of State Legislators." *Western Political Quarterly* 44, 2:445–56.

Treiman, Donald J. & Kermit Terrell. 1975. "Sex and the Process of Status Attainment: A Comparison of Working Women and Men." *American Sociological Review* 40:174–200.

Tucker H. & H. Ziegler. 1980. *Professionals Versus the Public: Attitudes, Communication, and Response in School Districts*. New York: Longman Group Ltd.

United Nations. 1991. *The World's Women 1970–1990 Trends and Statistics*. New York: United Nations Publications.

United Nations. 1965–1995. *Demographic Yearbook*. New York: United Nations Publications.

United Nations. 1972. *Statistical Yearbook*. Department of Economic and Social Information and Policy Analysis, Statistical Division, New York: United Nations Publishing.

United Nations. 1991. *Statistical Yearbook*. Department of Economic and Social Information and Policy Analysis, Statistical Division, New York: United Nations Publishing.

United Nations. 1992. *Abortion Policies: A Global Review*. New York: United Nations Publications.

United Nations Center for Social Development and Humanitarian Affairs. 1991. *Women in Decision-making, Greece*. New York: United Nations Publishing.

United States Bureau of Labor Statistics. 1980. *United States Department of Labor Directory of National Unions and Employee Associations*. Washington, DC: Bureau of Labor Statistics.

United States Bureau of Labor Statistics. 1989. *Monthly Labor Review*. Washington, DC: Bureau of Labor Statistics.

van Doorne-Huiskes, Anneke, Jacques van Hoof, & Ellie Roelofs, eds. 1995. *Women and the European Labour Market*. London: P. Chapman Publishers.

Verba, S. & N. Nie. 1972. *Participation in America: Political Democracy and Social Equality*. New York: Harper & Row.

Wahlke, John C. 1971. "Policy Demands and System Support: The Role of the Represented." *British Journal of Political Science* 1:271–90.

Walker, Nancy J. 1986. "Are Women More Peaceminded than Men?" Paper presented at the ECPR Conference, Gothenburg, Sweden, April 1986.

Walsh, Kenneth. 1985. *Trade Union Membership*. Luxembourg: Office for Official Publications of the European Community; Washington, DC: European Community Information Service.

Welch, Susan. 1977. "Women as Political Animals." *American Journal of Political Science* 21:711–30.

Welch, Susan. 1985. "Are Women More Liberal Than Men in the U.S. Congress?" *Legislative Studies Quarterly* 10:125–34.

Welch, Susan & Timothy Bledsoe. 1985. "Differences in Campaign Support for Male and Female Candidates." In *Research in Politics and Society*, eds. Glenna Spitze & Gwen Moore. Greenwich, CT: JAI Press.

Welch, Susan & John Hibbing. 1992. "Financial Conditions, Gender, and Voting in American Elections." *Journal of Politics* 54:197–213.

Welch, Susan & A. Karnig. 1979. "The Impact of Black Elected Officials on Urban Expenditures and Intergovernmental Revenues." In *Urban Policy*, ed. D. Marshall. Beverly Hills: Sage Publications.

Welch, Susan & Lee Sigelman. 1982. "Changes in Public Attitudes Toward Women in Politics." *Social Science Quarterly* 63:312–22.

Welch, Susan & Donley T. Studlar. 1990. "Multi-Member Districts and the Representation of Women: Evidence from Britain and the United States." *Journal of Politics* 52:391–412.

Werner, Emmy E. 1968. "Women in the State Legislatures." *Western Political Quarterly* 21:40–50.

White, Julie. 1980. *Women and Unions.* Ottawa: Canadian Government Publishing Center.

Wilcox, Clyde. 1994. "Why Was 1992 the 'Year of the Woman'? Explaining Women's Gains in 1992." In *The Year of the Women*, ed. E. A. Cook, S. Thomas & C. Wilcox. Boulder: Westview Press, Inc.

Wilensky, H. 1975. *Budgeting: A Comparative Theory of Budgetary Processes.* Boston: Little, Brown and Company.

Williams, Robert E. & Thomas R. Bagby. 1984. "The Legal Framework." In *Comparable Worth: Issues and Alternatives*, ed. E. R. Livernash. Washington, DC: Equal Employment Advisory Council.

Yoko, Nuita, Yamaguchi Mitsuko & Kubo Kimiko. 1994. "Japan, The U.N. Convention on Eliminating Discrimination Against Women and the Status of Women in Japan." In *Women and Politics Worldwide*, ed. B. Nelson & N. Chowdhury. New Haven: Yale University Press.

Zabalza, A. & Z. Tzannatos. 1985. "The Effect of Britain's Anti-Discriminatory Legislation on Relative Pay and Employment." *The Economic Journal* 95:679–99.

Index

abortion rights policy, 32, 36
Act No. 72–1143 on Equal Re-
    muneration for Men and
    Women (France), 67
Act on Equal Status Between the
    Sexes, 1978 (Norway), 62
Act on Equality in Work and
    Employment, 1979 (Portugal),
    57
"acting for" concept of represen-
    tation, 2–4
African American representation,
    8–10
Anti-Discrimination Act, 1974
    (Ireland), 54
apolitical, 15, 16, 23
Article 3 of the Basic Law (Ger-
    many), 64
Article 22–1b (Greece), 58
Article 37 (Italy), 58
Australia, 26, 78
Austria, 64–66, 72, 73, 101

Belgium, 48, 78
Britain, 40, 52–54, 71

Canada, 26, 48–52, 71
Canadian Human Rights Act, 52
Canadian Labour Code, 51, 52
Catholics/Catholic nations, 35,
    36, 46, 47, 53, 78, 80, 94–98,
    109–112
Central Arbitration Committee
    (Britain), 53
class-based representation, 11
collective bargaining, 39, 40, 43,
    59, 61, 99
Commonwealth nations, 48, 52
comparable worth, 44, 45, 49,
    62, 70, 99, 115
concurrence, between representa-
    tives and constituents, 6–8
congruence, between representa-
    tives and constituents, 5, 8
"critical level," of female repre-
    sentatives, 18, 24, 109

day care, 18, 31
democratic government, 2, 30
Denmark, 48, 63, 72, 73, 101,
    104

descriptive representation, 3, 4, 9, 17, 122
divorce/marriage policy, 32
domestic violence/rape policy, 32, 33

Education Amendments Act, 1972 (United States), 50
electoral systems, 14
eligibility pools, 14, 15
employment and wage protection policy, 19, 27, 30, 31, 33, 35, 39, 79–81, 84, 88, 89, 94–98, 104, 105, 120
Equal Employment Opportunity Commission EEOC (United States), 50
Equal Opportunities Commission (Sweden), 61
Equal Opportunities Ombudsman (Sweden), 61
equal opportunity for women in employment policy, 31
Equal Pay Act, 1963 (United States), 49
Equal Pay Act, 1970 (Britain), 53
Equal Pay Bill, 1972 (New Zealand), 55
Equal Pay Law, 1975 (Netherlands), 68
Equal Pay Law Committee (Netherlands), 68
Equal Remuneration Act, 1976 (Denmark), 63, 64
Equal Status Appeals Board (Norway), 63
Equal Status Commissioner (Norway), 62

Equal Status Council (Denmark), 63
Equal Treatment Commission (Austria), 66
Equal Treatment in Employment Law (Italy), 59
Equal Treatment Law (Austria), 66
equal wage policy, 29, 72, 77, 98–115, 120
Equal Work and Employment Commission (Portugal), 57
equality in education policy, 32
Equality of Treatment Board (Iceland), 62

family/child responsibility policy, 32, 33
female representation, 22–29
Finland, 48, 78, 84
formalistic models, 2, 3
France, 32, 48, 66, 67, 72, 73, 101

gender gap, 19
Germany, 27, 48, 64, 65, 72, 73
Government Service Equal Pay Act, 1960 (New Zealand), 55
Greece, 30, 43, 48, 58, 72, 78, 92, 96, 97, 112, 116
gross domestic product, 40, 93, 97, 109–113

heads of government, 35, 46, 88, 98 109, 111, 113, 116, 121
Human Rights Commission (Canada), 52

Iceland, 48, 60, 62, 72
incumbency advantage, 14

Ireland, 32, 48, 52–55, 71, 73, 101
Irish Employment Equality
    Agency, 55
Italy, 48, 56, 58–60, 72

Japan, 26, 48, 69, 70, 73, 101
job segregation, 32, 42, 44, 51,
    53, 62, 67, 68, 70, 73

Labor Standards Act of 1947
    (Japan), 69
Labor Standards Bureau (Japan),
    70
Latino representation, 10
Law 8 (Spain), 56, 57
Law 1414 (Greece), 58
Law Concerning Equal Treat-
    ment of Men and Women
    (Germany), 65
Law on the Equality of Women
    and Men, 1976 (Iceland), 62
left-wing parties, 14

maternity leave, 31, 32, 80
Ministry of Labour and Social
    Affairs (Germany), 65
minority representation, 8–11

National Commission for Equal
    Opportunities (Italy), 60
Netherlands, 27, 48, 64, 68, 69,
    72, 73
New Zealand, 26, 48, 52, 53, 55,
    71
Norway, 48, 60, 62, 63, 72, 96,
    101

parental leave, 31, 32, 80
Pitkin, Hanna, 2–4

political party influence, 23, 37,
    46, 92, 109–112, 116
Portugal, 30, 43, 48, 56, 57, 72,
    78, 92, 96, 97, 101, 112, 116
protective measures, 69, 84, 94,
    101, 120

representation theory, 2–12
responsiveness, of representa-
    tives, 2, 5–8, 10, 23
Roudy Law (France), 67

seniority, 18, 34, 50, 106, 114
sexual division of labor, 22
social policy, 19, 27, 30–33, 39,
    77, 79–81, 84–95, 97, 98, 120,
    122
Socialist party, 14, 37, 46
Spain, 30, 43, 48, 56, 57, 72, 78,
    92, 96, 97, 112, 116
"standing for" concept of repre-
    sentation, 2, 4, 9
Statute of Workers Article 28
    (Spain), 56
substantive representation, 4, 17,
    120, 122
Sweden, 48, 60, 61, 72, 73, 84,
    101
Swedish Act on Equality be-
    tween Men and Women at
    Work, 61
Switzerland, 48, 78
symbolic representation, 3, 4

union influence, 11, 38, 39, 46,
    86, 109–113
United States, 1, 11, 13, 15, 25,
    26, 34, 48, 49, 50, 73, 84

welfare state, 29, 40, 60
womens issues, 18, 19, 21, 22,
    25, 26, 114, 119–123
work of equal value, 44, 45, 50,
57–58, 62, 65–68, 72, 73, 99,
    106, 109, 115
Working Womens Welfare Act
    (Japan), 70

About the Author

VALERIE R. O'REGAN is Assistant Professor of Political Science at North Dakota State University. Her articles have appeared in various publications, and her research interests focus on women and politics.